YOU'VE GOT

Personality

An introduction to the personality types
described by Carl Jung and Isabel Myers

by Mary McGuiness

Published in Australia by

MaryMac Books

Contents

Acknowledgements:

The content of this book is based on the work of Carl Jung and Isabel Myers. The type descriptions contained in this book were compiled from data shared by several thousand workshop participants I have trained over the past 16 years. Thankyou to all of you who shared your personal stories with me. I am very grateful also to Noel Davis and Margaret Hartzler who shared their knowledge of type theory with me during those years and have inspired me to search for a deeper understanding. And, a special Thankyou to my children, Catherine and Damian, who have taught me so much about personality type and its value, and who encouraged me to finish this book. - Mary McGuiness

Published by:
MaryMac Books
P.O. Box 715
Cherrybrook NSW 2126
Australia
www.itd.net.au
Email: marymcg@itd.net.au

International Standards Book Number: 0-9751888-1-1

Front cover layout and design: Pixelcraft

The Myers-Briggs Type Indicator® and MBTI® are registered trademarks of the Myers-Briggs Type Indicator Trust in the USA and other countries.

Personality Differences

Have you ever wondered why you can relate easily to some people and not to others? Do you know why you find some people more attractive, or why some people seem to speak your language even at your first meeting? Do some things stress you while other people you know find them exciting or enjoyable?

You can find the answers to these questions by examining a few natural personality differences. We share a lot of very specific personality characteristics or *preferences* with some people, and so we find it easy to relate to them. Our natural preferences affect what we like and dislike, and may explain why certain things stress us. This book will explain some of these personality differences and will help you understand your needs, motivations, behaviour patterns, and how your personality has developed during your life. It will also give you insight into why and how other people are different from you, and will help you to appreciate those differences.

This personality theory is based on the work of the Swiss Psychiatrist Carl Jung (1875-1961). Jung noticed that much human behaviour that appears random actually follows clear and predictable patterns related to a few basic personality differences. In his book, *Psychological Types*, Jung described some of the personality differences in normal healthy people. These differences indicate our natural gifts and strengths. They influence the way we behave, communicate and interact in many daily situations in the workplace and at home.

Four Functions

Jung's theory of personality types focuses on two processes, Perception and Judgement:

Perception is the process of gathering information, through our senses or through intuition. The *Sensing* process focuses on concrete tangible data that is perceived when we see, touch, taste, hear and smell. *Intuition* perceives information as ideas and concepts, focusing on connections, possibilities, patterns and meaning.

Judgement refers to how we process information to make decisions. The two Judging processes involve weighing up information in a rational way. The *Thinking* function uses logic and analysis to make decisions. The *Feeling* function weighs values and relationships to make decisions.

These processes, Sensing, Intuition, Thinking and Feeling, indicate how we prefer to use our minds. They are called functions or mental processes.

Four Attitudes

Jung also described two different ways people focus their energy:
Extraversion is a preference for focusing on the external world of people, things or activity. People who prefer Extraversion will seek regular stimulation from the outer world.
Introversion is a preference for focusing on the inner world of ideas, thoughts and feelings. People preferring Introversion tend to want to spend a lot of time in quiet reflection.

Based on Jung's two processes of Judgment and Perception, Isabel Myers (1897-1980) and her mother Katharine Briggs (1875-1968) created a fourth dimension, called Judging and Perceiving. These preferences indicate whether a person's focus in the outer world is on making decisions (Judging), or on gathering information (Perceiving).

Extraversion, Introversion, Judging and Perceiving are referred to as Attitudes.

Preferences

Just as most people have a natural preference for left or right-handedness, so we have preferences or tendencies related to our personality. The table below outlines eight personality preferences. Each person is able to use and develop all eight preferences but will usually prefer one from each pair. The behaviours and abilities related to our natural preferences will develop quickly and easily in an environment that is positive and supportive. Behaviours and abilities that are related to preferences that are not natural for us will require more effort and may cause stress for us as they develop.

Remember:
- All people have preferences
- Preferences indicate our natural gifts
- Preference is not the same as skill
- Preferences are innate - we are born with them
- Personality type develops over the lifetime
- Personality type does not determine behaviour.

The Four Pairs of Preferences		
What is the direction and focus of your personal energy ?	**E Extraversion** ☐ A preference for the outer world of people, events, activity and things.	**I Introversion** ☐ A preference for the inner world of ideas, thoughts, feelings and impressions.
How do you prefer to gather information ?	**S Sensing** ☐ Focus on past or present experience, what is experienced through the senses.	**N iNtuition** ☐ Focus on patterns, future possibilities and the meaning behind ideas.
How do you prefer to make decisions ?	**T Thinking** ☐ Use logic to make decisions. Base decisions on laws and principles or logical analysis.	**F Feeling** ☐ Weigh values to make decisions. Decide what is most important for people.
How do you deal with the outer world ?	**J Judging** ☐ Prefer to be planned and organised in the outer world, seeking closure.	**P Perceiving** ☐ Prefer to be spontaneous and flexible in the outer world, ready to explore new options.

Behaviours related to the Eight Preferences

What is the direction and focus of your personal energy ?

Extraversion E ☐	**Introversion** I ☐
Outgoing, expressive	Reflective, quiet
Energised by interaction	Energised by being alone
Initiate conversation	Wait to be invited
Act before reflecting	Reflect before acting
Sociable - easy to get to know	Reserved - take time to get to know
Have many interests	Focus on a few things at depth
Need regular interaction	Need privacy for concentration
Interested more in external events	Interested more in internal reactions
Communicate more easily by talking	Communicate more easily by writing
Learn best by doing or interacting	Learn best by reading and reflecting

How do you prefer to gather information ?

Sensing S ☐	**iNtuition** N ☐
Perceive mainly through the 5 senses	Perceive mainly patterns and connections
Focus on facts and details	Focus on possibilities and hunches
Trust concrete experience	Trust theory and abstract concepts
Realistic and observant	Imaginative and innovative
Prefer practical matters	Prefer the imagination
Use a step-by-step approach	Use a random approach
Focus on the present or the past	Focus on the future
Seek stability	Seek change
Build up the big picture	Begin with the big picture
Need to see the parts to understand the whole	Need to see the whole to understand the parts

How do you prefer to make decisions ?

Thinking T ☐	**Feeling** F ☐
Use logic to make decisions	Use personal values to make decisions
Seek honesty and truth	Seek personal approval
Need to be competent	Need to be appreciated
Analyse and critique	Empathise
Firm and tough-minded	Persuasive and warm-hearted
Focus on justice and fairness	Focus on mercy and compassion
Questioning - focus on Why?	Accepting - focus on Who?
Seek logical reasons	Seek harmony with values and others
Focus on goals and tasks	Focus on people and relationships
Consider principles and consequences	Consider the impact on people

How much structure or flexibility do you need in the outer world ?

Judging J ☐	**Perceiving** P ☐
Prefer a definite order and structure	Flexible
Organised and planned	Adapt easily to change
Seek closure	Open-ended
Focus on reaching the goal	Focus on experiencing life
Like to control events	Like to respond to the moment
Make decisions quickly	Explore all the options before deciding
Systematic and methodical	Casual, easy-going
Comfortable with plans and timetables	Prefer to be spontaneous
Enjoy completing one project before starting another	Enjoy working on several projects at once
Punctual, meet deadlines easily	Energised by approaching deadlines

One preference from each pair is preferred and usually better developed.

My personality type preferences are: ___ ___ ___ ___

Personality Development

Skilful use of the functions takes practice. Jung believed that, although our functions are present at birth, they take time to develop. In a supportive environment, a child or adolescent will continually use the functions that feel natural, so these functions will develop quickly. They will usually spend little time using the functions that are not natural and so these will be slower to develop. Jung and Myers were both aware that we can use all of the functions but some functions are more important and there is a typical order in which they develop.

The usual pattern of development

The order in which the functions develop is different for each of the personality types. The table on the right indicates the typical order of development for each type. The approximate ages at which each function emerges are given below.

Infancy (0-6 years): A child will use all of the preferences, experimenting to see which ones are more comfortable and work better. The preference for E or I is usually obvious at this time. Some of the other preferences may also be observed.

Childhood (6-12 years): The Dominant function develops in the preferred world, E or I. It takes the lead in the personality.

Adolescence (13-20 years): The Auxiliary function develops in the opposite world to the Dominant function. It supports the Dominant function, providing a process to use in the less-preferred world. This means that if the Dominant function is extraverted the Auxiliary function will be introverted.

Early Adulthood (20-35 years): The Third (Tertiary) function develops. Myers believed that this function develops in the same world as the Auxiliary function. More recent research suggests that it most likely develops in the same world as the Dominant function.

Midlife (35-50 years): The Fourth function develops in your less-preferred world. This is usually the least developed of the four functions and the most likely to lose control when you are stressed. It is sometimes called the *Inferior* function. If this function is well-developed it can be used effectively and under control.

Integration (50+ years): Energy is spent integrating all of the functions, learning to use them appropriately.

Individuation - the journey to wholeness

Jung believed that we have an innate drive towards wholeness which calls us to develop the various aspects of our personality. During childhood and adolescence we direct our energy toward developing those preferences that feel most natural and comfortable for us. This gives us our personality style or type. As we move through adult life, the circumstances of life demand that we develop the opposite preferences in order to grow. The development of these opposite preferences often requires some effort and courage because we experience an awkwardness and clumsiness as we begin to use them. With practice we can develop the skills associated with these preferences and access more of our hidden potential.

The journey of adult life is an inner journey to find our deeper self. To do this we must let go of the conscious control of the Dominant and Auxiliary functions and allow the Third and Fourth functions to be developed and integrated into the personality. This allows the true self to emerge. Jung called this process *Individuation*.

The order of importance and the order of Development of the Functions

	1.	2.	3.	4.
ISTJ	Si	Te	Fi	Ne
ISFJ	Si	Fe	Ti	Ne
INTJ	Ni	Te	Fi	Se
INFJ	Ni	Fe	Ti	Se
ISTP	Ti	Se	Ni	Fe
INTP	Ti	Ne	Si	Fe
ISFP	Fi	Se	Ni	Te
INFP	Fi	Ne	Si	Te
ESTP	Se	Ti	Fe	Ni
ESFP	Se	Fi	Te	Ni
ENFP	Ne	Fi	Te	Si
ENTP	Ne	Ti	Fe	Si
ESTJ	Te	Si	Ne	Fi
ENTJ	Te	Ni	Se	Fi
ESFJ	Fe	Si	Ne	Ti
ENFJ	Fe	Ni	Se	Ti

1. Dominant   2. Auxiliary   3. Third   4. Fourth
e = external world   i = inner world

Example: ISTJ and ENFP

ISTJ children will usually be quiet, practical, organised and responsible. They notice facts and details and respect rules and authority. During adolescence, as Thinking develops, the ISTJ will approach decisions and tasks with logic, organising the outer world systematically to maintain order. ISTJs will often mistrust intuition and keep their feelings hidden. In adult life, as the Feeling function develops, they may experience overwhelming emotions and deep, compassion. The most challenging area of development for them is often learning to trust inspirations and hunches that come from Intuition, and this may not develop fully until after the age of 40.

ENFP children will trust their intuition and imagination. They often miss details and pay little attention to practical issues. During their adolescence, as the Feeling function develops, they will reflect more on their deep values and may question rules and authority. They often have difficulty managing time and asserting themselves, preferring to keep the peace. In adult life, as the Thinking function develops, they will often enjoy approaching tasks and decisions in a more logical way and be more comfortable expressing their opinions. The most challenging area of development for them will be the Sensing function. They may have difficulty with practical issues, and with facing reality and living in the present moment.

Good personality development

Good personality development does not require that you develop all of the functions equally. It requires that you have well-developed Dominant and Auxiliary functions, and that you can use the other functions when appropriate. In a person with normal, healthy development the Dominant and the Auxiliary functions will probably always remain better developed than the Third and Fourth functions.

The Eight Jungian Functions

Each of the functions, Sensing, Intuition, Thinking and Feeling, can be used in the internal world or the external world. When a function is used in the external world it will be expressed differently to a function that operates in the internal world. Carl Jung described eight functions or cognitive processes (see below). It is possible for a person to develop each of these eight functions, but some will be more natural for each type and will develop more easily.

Each personality type has an innate preference for one of the perceiving functions and one of the judging functions. See the table opposite for details. One of these functions will be called the Dominant function, and the other is the supporting or Auxiliary function. If you prefer Extraversion, your Dominant function will be the one you use in the external world. If you prefer Introversion, your Dominant function will be the one you use in the inner world.

The **Dominant Function** operates in your preferred world and usually develops during childhood. It takes the lead in your personality and has the strongest influence throughout your life. The **Auxiliary Function** supports the Dominant and has an important role in providing balance for the personality. It develops in the opposite world to the Dominant and comes from a different dichotomy. So, for example, if the Dominant function is an Extraverted Perceiving function, the Auxiliary function will be an Introverted Judging function. This provides balance on the E-I and J-P dimensions.

Example: For the ENTJ, Intuition is introverted and Thinking is extraverted. (See table opposite). Since this type prefers Extraversion, Thinking is the Dominant function and Intuition is the Auxiliary. The ENTJ uses Thinking (Logic) to organise the outer world, and uses Intuition in the inner world to deal with concepts and to vision the future.

The Perceiving functions

Se extraverted Sensing
Sensory experience

Focuses on
- Details perceived through the five senses
- Sensory stimulation from the external world
- What is experienced in the present
- What is real and tangible

Extraverted Sensing is the Dominant function for ESFP and ESTP, and the Auxiliary function for ISFP and ISTP.

This preference leads people to focus on reality in the present, what they can see, touch, taste hear and smell. Their observations are detailed and accurate. They are realistic and spend energy enjoying the present moment, doing things and having fun. Others see them as realists. They may have difficulty trusting the imagination.

Si introverted Sensing
Sensory memory

Focuses on
- Impression made by past sensory experience
- Inner reality and body sensations
- What is known from experience
- Comparing the present with past experience

Introverted Sensing is the Dominant function for ISFJ and ISTJ, and the Auxiliary function for ESFJ and ESTJ.

This preference leads people to compare present reality to the stored impressions from the past. They trust what they know from experience and so will tend to resist change until they are convinced that it is useful and will work better. Other people will often see them as quiet observers. They may have difficulty seeing new ways and possibilities.

Ne extraverted Intuition
Exploring possibilities

Focuses on
- Generating possiblities for the future
- Patterns and connections
- New ideas and new ways of doing things
- What is triggered in the imagination

Extraverted Intuition is Dominant function for ENFP and ENTP, and the Auxillary function for INFP and INTP.

People who extravert Intuition focus on what could be, rather than what is. The external stimulus triggers the imagination to see many new and different possiblities. They enjoy brainstorming and finding new ways. Other people often see them as change agents. They may have difficulty dealing with concrete reality and completing tasks.

Ni introverted Intuition
Visionary insight

Focuses on
- A vision of what is possible
- Goals for the future
- Symbols and images from the unconscious
- Whole patterns and systems

Introverted Intuition is the Dominant function for INFJ and INTJ, and the Auxiliary function for ENFJ and ENTJ.

People who introvert Intuition see things in symbolic ways. They have a rich abstract imagination and often express this through poetry or metaphors. They focus their energy towards their perceived goal. Other people often see them as visionary, insightful and innovators. They may have difficulty seeing things as they really are in the external world.

Type Dynamics

Type	Functions	Type	Functions
ISTJ	SiTe	ISFJ	SiFe
ESTJ	SiTe	ESFJ	SiFe
ISTP	SeTi	ISFP	SeFi
ESTP	SeTi	ESFP	SeFi
INTJ	NiTe	INFJ	NiFe
ENTJ	NiTe	ENFJ	NiFe
INTP	NeTi	INFP	NeFi
ENTP	NeTi	ENFP	NeFi

The Dominant function is the function you use in your preferred world.

The Judging functions

Te extraverted Thinking ☐
Logical outcomes

Focuses on
- Tasks - what needs to be done
- Goals, priorities, policies and laws
- Logical organisation
- Competency and efficiency in what they do

Extraverted Thinking is the Dominant function for ESTJ and ENTJ, and the Auxiliary function for ISTJ and INTJ.

People who extravert Thinking are pragmatic, applied thinkers, concerned with goals and outcomes. They organise the external world into logical systems. They analyse issues out loud and use logic to convince others. Others may see them as task-focused. They may have some difficulty understanding and relating to the people working on the task.

Fe extraverted Feeling ☐
Harmonizing people

Focuses on
- The needs of people
- Creating harmony and pleasing others
- Behaving appropriately in a situation
- Connecting with particular people or groups

Extraverted Feeling is the Dominant function for ESFJ and ENFJ, and the Auxiliary function for ISFJ and INFJ.

People who extravert Feeling try to create harmony at work and at home. They thrive on personal affirmation and approval. They often neglect their own needs and may lose themselves meeting the needs of others. Others may see them as people-centred. They may have difficulty handling conflict or seeing the logical consequences of decisions.

Ti introverted Thinking ☐
Internal analysis

Focuses on
- The *why* of what is being done
- Building frameworks and models in the inner world
- Clarifying and making precise
- Competency in analysing, classifying and sorting

Introverted Thinking is the Dominant function for ISTP and INTP, and the Auxiliary function for ESTP and ENTP.

People who introvert Thinking are more concerned with the thinking and the principles involved than with outcomes. They check new information against their internal framework or model. They often question established ways of thinking. Others may see them as skeptical. They may have difficulty with relationships and the pragmatics of their thinking.

Fi introverted Feeling ☐
Universal values

Focuses on
- Universal values such as peace, love and freedom
- Defending people or causes
- Behaving in ways consistent with their internal values
- Making decisions that are value-consistent

Introverted Feeling is the Dominant function for ISFP and INFP, and the Auxiliary function for ESFP and ENFP.

People who introvert Feeling evaluate things with their own internal values more than the values of the group or society. They are nonconformists. They feel for the world and may be overwhelmed by feelings of sadness, joy, grief or guilt. Others may see them as nonconformist or stubborn. They may have difficulty expressing their values with clarity.

Communication Styles

Everything we do or say communicates a message to others. Communication may be verbal, written or nonverbal through mannerisms, actions and expressions. Each preference in our personality type will have an impact on communication. When we communicate in words, spoken or written, our communication style will use one or more of the eight of the functions, described on pages 6 and 7.

The Functions in Attitude

Each personality type includes two functions. One is used in the outer world (external) and one in the internal world. The function you use in the outer world is the one that will tend to take the lead in communication. Therefore, the four primary communication styles are Se, Ne, Te and Fe.

If two people share the same communication style it is likely that their conversation will flow easily and each will feel heard and understood. If two people with different communication styles try to communicate the interaction may feel awkward or frustrating, as if they are speaking different languages. Their communication will improve if one or both shift so that they are using the same communication style. This may happen unconsciously, or one person may consciously choose to shift from his or her natural communication style to another style which mirrors the language of the other person.

Example: ENFP and ISTJ

When an ENFP speaks to an ISTJ they may experience some difficulty understanding each other at first. The ENFP prefers extraverted Intuition and so will want to explore the topic through brainstorming, finding connections between many ideas. They will usually not want to make a decision or bring closure to the topic until they have explored enough ideas and generated many possibilities. On the other hand an ISTJ prefers extraverted Thinking and will want to come to closure quickly. ISTJs will analyse the topic in a logical way, using the available data and may be frustrated by the ENFP's focus on future possibilities rather than on present reality. For the communication to flow well, one or both will need to shift to a different communication style.

Communication Style	Types
(Se) extraverted Sensing	ESFP, ESTP, ISFP, ISTP
(Ne) extraverted Intuition	ENFP, ENTP, INFP, INTP
(Te) extraverted Thinking	ESTJ, ENTJ, ISTJ, INTJ
(Fe) extraverted Feeling	ESFJ, ENFJ, ISFJ, INFJ

Communicating with Perceiving functions

How extraverted Sensing communicates:	To communicate with extraverted Sensing:
Shares facts and details	Focus on real life experience or examples.
Focuses on the present moment	Be specific - colour, time, shape, sound, taste etc.
Speaks in literal language and gives detailed instructions	Finish your sentences and indicate when changing topics.
Uses words like - real, sense, do, fun, facts.	Start with details and build the big picture.
	Give specific instructions.
The challenge: To see the big picture and how things connect. To see possibilities beyond what is observable.	

How extraverted Intuition communicates:	To communicate with extraverted Intuition:
Shares ideas, concepts and theory, the big picture.	Allow them to explore ideas and possibilities freely.
Focuses on brainstorming future possibilities.	Look beyond the facts to see the implications.
Speaks in global language, generalisations, metaphors.	Don't overwhelm them with too many facts.
Uses words like - imagine, dreams, possible, ideas.	Start with the big picture and show how facts relate to it.
	Give broad instructions without specifying each step.
The challenge: To be specific and look at factual data. To focus on reality and experience.	

The E-I Attitudes

The E-I attitudes often influence how you communicate, the energy and enthusiasm with which you express your ideas and feelings, and who initiates communication.

People who prefer **Extraversion** often initiate conversations and express their thoughts and feelings readily. They often need to talk out their ideas in order to gain clarity, so they may change their viewpoint as the conversation progresses. They process itheir ideas out loud. The challenge for people who prefer Extraversion is to spend more time reflecting on their often busy lifestyle. Without reflection an extraverted life may lack clear direction.

People who prefer **Introversion** will often wait to be invited into conversations. They usually process their thoughts and feelings internally and may not express them to others. This process is internal and is not usually obvious to others. Sometimes they rehearse a conversation in their minds and believe they have had the conversation with the other person. The challenge for people who prefer Introversion is to speak out their ideas and feelings so that other people can understand them, and so that they have an impact in the external world.

The J-P Attitudes

The J-P attitudes influence the focus of communication - is the communication focused on an outcome or a goal, or is it open-ended, desiring to share information and experience?

People who prefer **Perceiving** will tend to communicate in an open-ended way, gathering and sharing information. They will make few judgements and will not usually seek closure on a topic, preferring to explore. If you are listening to a person with a preference for Perceiving as they express an opinion, don't assume they have made a decision. They will usually share a lot of information or ideas before they make a decision, and then are still open to change.

People who prefer **Judging** will usually be more definite and decisive as they communicate. They express opinions, make judgements about the topic and seek a definite conclusion or closure. They often state an opinion hoping for some debate or a new viewpoint. Once they have reached a decision they are usually reluctant to change it. If you are communicating with a person with a preference for Judging, don't assume that they don't want to hear your opinion. And, make sure you have all the necessary information before you decide.

Communicating with Judging functions

How extraverted Thinking communicates:	To communicate with extraverted Thinking:
Debates issues using logic to convince others	Debate and challenge their ideas.
Orders or sequences ideas	Present facts and ideas logically.
Speaks out logical thoughts	Be direct - state the outcomes you envisage.
Uses words like -think, criteria, logical, outcome, priority.	Share feelings but don't lose control of your emotions.
	Affirm their ideas and competence.
The challenge: To understand the needs of people.	
To know how to influence people to accept their ideas.	

How extraverted Feeling communicates:	To communicate with extraverted Feeling:
Connects with people through words and body language.	Use personal language to establish rapport.
Focuses on feelings and the impact on people.	Explain the benefits for people.
Speaks in personal language to create harmony.	Be supportive and tactful when giving feedback.
Uses words like: value, relationship, personal, feel, friendly.	Acknowledge that feelings and relationships are important.
	Affirm them for their valuable contribution.
The challenge: To express their own views, even when it may create disharmony. To detach from their emotions.	

Stress and the Inferior Function

What is Stress?

Many external events or people may cause us to feel stressed, but these external stimuli are not the stress. Stress comes from within. It is the bodily or physical discomfort we feel in response to these external events or people. Sometimes this discomfort may be pleasant, exciting or challenging, such as competing for an award. Sometimes this discomfort may be unpleasant or distressful, such as conflict at work or financial difficulty. We can take steps to reduce the distress we experience, but first we need to identify what is triggering the stressful response and to understand why we respond the way we do.

Personality differences have a major impact on the way we experience stress and on how we respond to it. Some people or situations may be a trigger for you to experience anxiety, fear, guilt or powerlessness. Another person may actually enjoy that same experience. Understanding your personality type will give you insight into why some things stress you and what you can do about it. You can take steps to eliminate the stress from your life, or change the behaviour that may be causing it, or change the way you respond to it.

The Inferior Function

For each of the personality types, the Fourth function is the one most likely to lead to stressful situations, although the Tertiary function can also contribute at times. The Fourth function is called the *Inferior function* when it is out of control. It is more likely to get out of control when a person is under pressure from some external source, or is sick, tired, or under the influence of drugs. As long as this function remains poorly developed, its behaviour will be childish or primitive and the person will be defensive about its functioning.

When the inferior function takes control a person will often be moody, oversensitive to criticism, emotionally charged and unable to discuss things rationally. Because it is usually poorly developed it remains mostly in the unconscious. It therefore provides a strong connection to our unconscious world. This hidden world may contain repressed memories or fears, and those aspects of ourselves that we have not dealt with and would rather hide. And, it may also contain untapped potential, abilities and talents we have yet to discover. When the inferior function gets out of control some of these hidden things may come to the surface. This provides us with an opportunity to deal with these issues so that we no longer fear them. So, the inferior function plays and essential part in the growth and development of the personality.

How to deal with the Inferior Function

- Move back into your preferred world by using your Dominant or Tertiary function.
- Give yourself more time. The Inferior function is slower than the Dominant.
- Look at yourself with a sense of humour!
- Recognise that some things may be more difficult for you because of your personality type.
- Don't use your Inferior function when you are stressed.
- Be humble. Ask for help if you need it.
- Play! Take time to develop your fourth function when you are not stressed.
- Nurture the whole person - mind, body, emotions, spirit.

Behaviours you may observe when the Inferior function is in control.

When extraverted Sensing (Se) is Inferior:
May become over emotional or depressed
May be overwhelmed by facts they can't shut out
May seek non-stop stimulation
May over organise the outer world

When introverted Sensing (Si) is Inferior:
May ignore bodily needs for sleep, food
May become obsessive about caring for the body
May focus on irrelevant details
May become depressed and withdrawn

When extraverted Intuition (Ne) is Inferior:
May miss facts and details
May become confused or impulsive
May have difficulty finding solutions to a problem
May focus on negative possibilities

When introverted Intuition (Ni) is Inferior:
May become anxious and fear the future
May experience inner confusion and hopelessness
May experience depression
May lose physical mobility

When extraverted Thinking (Te) is Inferior
May become controlling and rigid in their thinking
May judge themselves or others to be incompetent
May fear losing control
May blame others and be destructively critical

When introverted Thinking (Ti) is Inferior:
May have negative thoughts about self and others
May shut down emotionally
May draw unrealistic conclusions
May be unable to think clearly or grasp concepts

When extraverted Feeling (Fe) is Inferior:
May become over emotional or sentimental
May be insensitive to other people
May be oversensitive or feel unappreciated
May find it difficult to express feelings

When introverted Feeling (Fi) is Inferior:
May become too focused on their inner feelings
May feel overwhelmed by emotions
May be oversensitive to criticism
May feel alone, worthless or incompetent

The Four Temperament Groups

Throughout history people have tried to understand and to describe human personality. One of the earliest descriptions was the temperament patterns described by the Greek scholar Hippocrates in 450 B.C. He described four basic patterns in human nature that determine our behaviour. These were called Sanguine, Melancholic, Phlegmatic and Choleric.

In the book *Please Understand Me* (1984), David Keirsey and Marilyn Bates described a modern version of temperament theory. They named these four temperament patterns Guardian, Artisan, Catalyst and Rational. They also described the relationship between the four temperaments and the sixteen personality types described by Isabel Myers. While these two theories come out of different histories and focus on different aspects of human nature, together they give a rich account of personality differences and help to explain the behaviour of people.

For each of the temperament groups Keirsey and Bates described particular needs that drive our behaviour. The behaviours that people take on are designed to ensure that these different needs are met.

Each temperament relates to four personality types:

Guardian:	ESFJ, ESTJ, ISFJ, ISTJ
Artisan:	ESFP, ESTP, ISFP, ISTP
Idealist:	ENFP, ENFJ, INFP, INFJ
Rational:	ENTP, ENTJ, INTP, INTJ

Guardian - Stabilizer (SJ)

Responsible, dependable
Focuses on the past, the way things have been done
Wants security, routine and predictability
Enjoys being of service
Saves and conserves
Logistical, practical
Values rules and authority
Trusts what is known from experience
Enjoys ceremonies, awards and prizes
Works to maintain institutions and order
Attracted to business or service industries

Needs:	Structure and order
	Belonging
	Responsibility
	Duty

Dislikes:	Disorganisation
	Lack of respect for authority

Idealist - Catalyst (NF)

Imaginative, innovative
Focuses on the future
Wants approval, harmony and cooperation
Catalyst for growth and development
Authentic, empathic
Romantic idealists
Has a strong personal code of ethics
Trusts inspirations and imagination
Enjoys helping others achieve their potential
Works to develop the potential in others
Attracted to working with people

Needs:	Meaning
	Identity
	Harmony
	Uniqueness

Dislikes:	Insincerity
	Disharmony

Artisan - Improvisor (SP)

Realistic, factual
Focuses the present
Wants immediate feedback
Natural negotiator and troubleshooter
Spontaneous, acts on impulses
Likes variety
Likes movement and hands-on activity
Optimistic
Enjoys fun and being playful
Work is often tactical - gets the job done
Attracted to active, physical work

Needs:	Freedom
	Action
	Fun
	To make an impression

Dislikes:	Rules and Hierarchy
	Routine

Rational - Theorist (NT)

Analytical, inventive
Focuses on the future
Self-critiquing, sets own standards
Independent thinker
Seeks justice and fairness
Asks Why? Why not? What if?
Likes models and theories
Values knowledge and understanding
Enjoys researching and problem-solving
Work often involves strategic planning and design
Attracted to science, technology and research

Needs:	Competence
	Intellectual freedom
	Mastery
	Achievement

Dislikes:	Incompetence
	Being told what to think

ESFP

Order of Functions:	Dominant	Se
	Auxiliary	Fi
	Tertiary	Te
	Inferior	Ni
Temperament:	Artisan (SP)	

Strengths

ESFPs are realistic, entertaining, honest and accommodating. They are fun-loving and humorous, and seek constant action and stimulation. They are natural negotiators and are good at motivating others and encouraging positive attitudes. ESFPs like to do several things at once and thrive in a crisis. They are adaptable and spontaneous, quick to size up a situation and deal with it. They need action and freedom in life and work.

The Dominant function of the ESFP is extraverted Sensing. This enables them to live in the moment and to absorb a lot of detailed information from the world around them. The supporting function of the ESFP is introverted Feeling, so they base their important decisions on deep personal values. They like to have lots of people around to interact with and have the ability to make them laugh.

Potential difficulties

The less-preferred functions of the ESFP are extraverted Thinking and introverted Intuition. ESFPs are often restless and may act before thinking an idea through. If they are bored they may quickly lose interest and they may begin many tasks but not complete them. ESFPs are not naturally organised so, if they lack discipline, they may not achieve what they want in life. They may have difficulty seeing the big picture. ESFPs may become confused with too many options and may find it difficult to assert themselves, wanting to please others.

Communication

The extraverted Sensing of ESFPs focuses on facts, details and reality in the present situation. They notice and remember a lot of detail, including body language, but get bored with a lot of detail from others. They dislike long explanations or lectures, preferring to get to the point quickly.

ESFPs are confident, enthusiastic and entertaining, and are comfortable sharing jokes, stories, anecdotes and humour. They prefer honest, straightforward communication. Their language tends to be realistic, friendly and literal. They may have difficulties with symbols and metaphors. Since their Feeling function is introverted they may find it difficult to say what they really feel. If you want to change their ideas or behaviour appeal to their values and negotiate, or just ask.

Relationships

ESFPs want a relationship that is warm, smooth, trouble-free and playful. In a relationship they value honesty and a sense of humour and want to be trusted. They also want physical expressions of affection. They are very sensitive to other people's feelings and will usually try hard to please others and maintain harmony. They get to know people quickly.

ESFPs usually have lots of friends but may not feel close to anyone and may feel lonely. They process their feelings internally, so they usually find it difficult to express feelings out loud, but they are very clear about what they value. They will usually avoid conflict until someone violates one of their deeper values.

Learning

ESFPs are realistic and practical. They learn more by doing than by listening and reading. They perceive information through their extraverted sensing, gathering detailed information through what they see, touch, taste, hear or smell. In a classroom they become bored if they don't have something to do and may become distracted and disruptive. ESFPs want to learn quickly and want learning to be fun. The content needs to be related to real life experiences with practical outcomes. ESFPs learn best in a supportive, interactive environment.

ESFPs enjoy practical subjects with hands-on learning and subjects where there is a very clear rule structure, such as French. They often enjoy performing, music, singing, dance or sport. They will read about things that interest them, such as stories with lots of action or books on how things work or realistic stories about people. They may find school difficult because they get bored with theory, too many details and too much talk. They may find essay writing difficult and may have difficulty when asked to explore the meaning of something or to imagine something they have not experienced.

At Work

At work ESFPs like a challenge and enjoy a crisis. They like opportunities for troubleshooting and have a strong desire to make a difference in the world. ESFPs can work in a structure as long as there is some freedom within it. They need physical freedom, flexibility, variety and the opportunity to be spontaneous at work. Their need for action may sometimes be mistaken for a need for closure. ESFPs get bored with routine and will usually find some way to create excitement and fun.

ESFPs focus on outcomes. They will often negotiate to get what they want and may step outside boundaries or rules. ESFPs are not usually impressed by rules, hierarchy, position or status. They often ignore rules if the rules don't make sense to them or if the rules conflict with their values. They won't necessarily break the rules but like to know that they have the freedom to do so. If they can't see the point in doing something they are unlikely to finish it.

Careers

ESFPs are often found in careers that involve trouble-shooting, mediation, negotiation or physical activity. This may include sales, technicians, maintenance work, trades, small business owners, child care, travel, recreation, marketing, sport, production, security and performing arts.

Team Role

As team members ESFPs add fun and encouragement. They like a lot of contact with people and are good at motivating them and creating a relaxed harmonious work team. Though they need variety, they like to have enough routine in their work so that they can concentrate on the people. They prefer short term projects and then they want to move on. They may at times have trouble staying focused and may have difficulty meeting deadlines.

Leadership Style

As managers or supervisors the ESFPs will focus on people and on creating harmony in the team. They are not usually authoritarian when in a leadership role, preferring to allow team members to have some freedom. They will often start a project and then find someone who has the skills to keep it going while they move on to something new.

The strengths of the ESFPs are their ability to motivate and encourage team members and to allow the team to have fun while they get the job done. Difficulties may occur if they become too distracted or too friendly and lose sight of the outcome or the deadline.

Stress for the ESFP

Causes of stress
The main causes of stress for the ESFP are loss of freedom and being alone. They dislike being tied down or controlled by people or deadlines and usually dislike long-term projects. The ESFPs need for freedom means that they may easily become stressed by situations or people who are inflexible and may find it difficult to stay within financial constraints.

Much of the stress of ESFPs comes from using their less-preferred functions, Intuition and Thinking. Having too much information, too many options or too many things to do at once may lead to confusion and they may forget something important like where they parked the car. They may be stressed by conflict in relationships, by people who are narrow-minded or critical, or people who lack common sense. They will be stressed by people who can't make effective decisions or won't take the necessary action to achieve what they want.

Behaviour under stress
When stressed ESFPs may feel vulnerable and upset, and may see the situation as worse than it really is. They may fear failure and worry about what others think of them. They may withdraw and feel anxious or depressed, or they may express their anger and move on. ESFPs under stress often lose spontaneity, become confused and feel unappreciated or bored, which may lead to laziness or disruptive behaviour. If their inferior introverted Intuition takes over they may have an unrealistic fear of what might go wrong. In some cases ESFPs may have a sudden attraction to mystical or religious experience or cults where people seem to have fun.

If people do not deal with serious stress they may engage in unhealthy psychological games to reduce the effects of stress. An ESFP who is not coping with stress may resort to blackmail games such as tantrums or violent outbursts, risky behaviour, boredom or depression. The unconscious reasons for this behaviour are to experience excitement and freedom, or to punish the person who has taken away their freedom. The long term effect of this behaviour is that they will often have their freedom taken away.

How to reduce stress
The ESFP will often use physical activity, fun, risk taking or new experiences, to reduce stress. They will usually seek the company of other people, preferring interaction to being alone. It is helpful for them to check the facts and be realistic about the situation, take time to plan, then use their internal values to decide what is the appropriate action, before they act. To be healthy and manage their stress it is essential that the ESFPs honour their basic need for freedom and action.

Leisure and Recreation
ESFPs are fun-loving and entertaining, preferring informal social events. They look for excitement and interaction and lose interest if they are not actively involved. They often enjoy the outdoors or activities that use up energy, many engaging in team sports or sometimes extreme sports like snow-boarding or parachuting. ESFPs may do some things alone like motor-bike riding, horse riding, surfing or sailing, enjoying the sensing aspects of the experience. They often like music, dance, travel, shopping and playing with children or animals.

ESFPs tend to read real life stories more than fantasy, and like stories with a lot of movement and interaction. They tend to prefer action movies, comedy such as the Marx Brothers, or real life stories about people struggling to overcome problems, such as documentaries about explorers. For the ESFP life has to be fun. They will say things like "You're here for a good time, not a long time. So, make the most of it."

ESFP Development

Childhood (6 - 12 years)
ESFP children are usually playful and interactive, interested in everyone and everything. The Dominant function of ESFPs is extraverted Sensing and develops during childhood. ESFP children are constantly active, interacting with people and things, and taking in vast amounts of facts and details through their senses. They are active, want constant stimulation and become bored quickly if they don't have something to do. They will put a lot of energy into an activity until they lose interest. ESFPs interpret language and instructions literally and trust what is real. They are humorous, like to be in the limelight and want to have fun.

Favourite activities for ESFP children often include sports such as hockey, swimming, athletics; outdoor activities and team games; collecting toys, rocks or cards about heroes; comedy movies; assembling mechanical things or Lego; playing with computer games or transformer toys; practical jokes and magic tricks; acting, singing or playing a musical instrument. They prefer activities that involve interacting with people, animals or things.

Adolescence (13 - 20 years)
During adolescence ESFPs will spend time reflecting on the things they value as they develop introverted Feeling. They make their decisions using personal values and process these internally. They often find it difficult to express their deeper feelings and may appear shy. They are honest and sensitive to other people's pain, and willingly help their friends deal with problems. ESFPs need a lot of emotional support. They also need freedom and will resist control. They respond positively to guidance from adults who understand them and encourage them to be themselves. They may have difficulty asserting themselves and often use humour to avoid conflict. ESFPs usually have an active social life and enjoy activities like sport, music or dance. They may find school frustrating because of the focus on theory rather than practical work.

Early Adulthood (20 - 35 years)
During this period the Third function, extraverted Thinking, emerges. The fun-loving personality of the ESFP continues throughout adulthood. As the Thinking emerges ESFPs will often become more assertive, more logical in making their decisions and less concerned about offending others. They may even appear aggressive as they begin to take charge of their own lives and feel a greater sense of freedom to be themselves. Some ESFPs at this time will look for new challenges in work or in the academic field. They may find themselves setting up new business ventures or beginning some serious academic study. They will usually become more confident in expressing their opinions and making decisions.

Midlife (35 - 55 years)
At midlife ESFPs develop introverted Intuition. The fun-loving interactive style of the ESFP continues, but now they will be more comfortable spending time alone reflecting. Their inner reflections are times of inspiration where they will focus on possibilities and visions for the future. They will be more interested in big picture concepts and theories. They will pay less attention to details and practical realities and may even find themselves daydreaming and forgetting things. They may begin to focus on appreciating symbols and the meaning behind what is real. ESFPs may feel drawn to dream work or meditation as they explore their inner Intuition. The creativity of ESFPs may increase at this time as they become more innovative.

ESTP

Order of Functions:	Dominant	Se
	Auxiliary	Ti
	Tertiary	Fe
	Inferior	Ni
Temperament:	Artisan (SP)	

Strengths

ESTPs are lively, realistic, pragmatic and fun-loving. They value truth and honesty and need constant action and stimulation. They are adaptable and spontaneous, quick to size up a situation and deal with it. They seek constant action and freedom in life and work. Their attitude is usually that they can do anything.

The Dominant function of the ESTP is extraverted Sensing. This enables them to live in the moment and to absorb a lot of detailed information from the world around them. The supporting function of the ESTP is introverted Thinking. This means they will tend to base their decisions on internal logic, They are resourceful and can improvise, making them good problem solvers and negotiators. They are motivated by a crisis and can think on their feet.

Potential difficulties

The less-preferred functions of ESTPs are extraverted Feeling and introverted Intuition. They may have difficulty seeing the big picture and may become confused if there are too many options. At times they may not be aware that their words or action offend others. ESTPs are often restless and may act before thinking an idea through. If they are bored they may quickly lose interest and they may begin many tasks but not complete them. ESTPs are not naturally organised. If they lack discipline they may not achieve what they want in life.

Communication

The extraverted Sensing of the ESTP focuses on facts, details and reality in the present situation. They notice and remember a lot of detail but get bored with a lot of detail from others They dislike long explanations, preferring to get to the point quickly. ESTPs are good at reading body language and listening to their gut feelings.

ESTPs like feedback to be immediate, honest and direct. They like to debate ideas related to concrete information. And, they like to deal with a problem and then move on. They are often natural negotiators. ESTP language tends to be realistic, impersonal and literal. When questioned they will churn things over and question whether they are right or wrong. If you want to change their ideas or behaviour give them logical reasons and negotiate.

Relationships

ESTPs usually have lots of friends but may have difficulty forming intimate relationships and may feel lonely. People may find it hard to get close to them or may think they don't have feelings. They will often ignore social role expectations. ESTP women often feel more at home in the company of males.

In a relationship ESTPs seek someone to share their thoughts and high energy level; a friend who can handle their fragile and sensitive side and not leave. The Feeling function is not familiar to them and so they usually keep their feelings to themselves. If a relationship gets into difficulties they will try to fix it. But they find it difficult to stay in a relationship if they are not happy.

Learning

ESTPs learn more by doing than by listening and reading. Their extraverted Sensing collects detailed information through what they see, touch, taste, hear or smell. ESTPs are often curious to know how things work and like to solve problems. They want to learn quickly and in a classroom may become bored if they don't have something to do. If they are bored they may become easily distracted and disruptive. ESTPs need regular interaction and a teacher who is competent or they quickly lose interest.

ESTPs usually enjoy practical subjects with hands-on learning and subjects where there is a very clear rule structure, such as French and Chemistry. They often enjoy music or sport. They will read only if the subject interests them. Often this will be adventure stories with lots of movement or books on how things work. As children they often find school difficult because they get bored with theory, too many details and too much talk from the teacher. Some ESTPs may find essay writing difficult and may have difficulty when asked to explore the meaning of something or to imagine something they have not experienced. They would prefer to talk about the reality.

At Work

At work ESTPs like a challenge and enjoy a crisis. They are lateral thinkers and prefer to have lots of things to do and problems to solve. They need physical freedom, flexibility, variety and the opportunity to be spontaneous. Their need for quick action in a situation may be mistaken for a need for closure. ESTPs get bored with routine and will often find some way to interrupt it. They can work in a structured situation as long as there is freedom within it.

ESTPs focus on outcomes. They will go to great lengths to get what they want and may step outside boundaries or rules. ESTPs are not usually impressed by rules, hierarchy, status or position. They will often ignore rules if they can't see the logic in them. They won't necessarily break the rules but like to know that they have the freedom to do so. If they can't see the point in doing something they are unlikely to finish it.

Careers

ESTPs are often found in jobs or careers that involve trouble-shooting, mediation, negotiation or physical activity. This may include such areas as technicians, maintenance work, trades, small business owners, entrepreneurs, recreation, marketing, sport, travel, production, security and performing arts.

Team Role

As team members ESTPs add fun and clarity of ideas. They like to work in a team that has clear targets. ESTPs are very creative situationally. They gather a lot of data and use the data to find the new ideas to solve problems. Once a problem is solved they want to move on. Many ESTPs stay in a job for only one or two years. They may at times be disruptive or irreverent and may have difficulty meeting deadlines.

Leadership Style

As managers or supervisors ESTPs will usually focus on the bottom line and will make sure the job gets done. They are not authoritarian when in a leadership role, preferring to allow people to have some freedom. They will often start a project and then find someone who has the skills to keep it going while they move on to something new.

The strengths of the ESTPs are their ability to gather and store a lot of information, to initiate projects and to facilitate the team throughout the project. Difficulties may occur if they act without enough data, if they don't meet deadlines or if they are not sensitive to other people's feeling.

Stress for the ESTP

Causes of stress
The main causes of stress for the ESTP are loss of freedom or the opposite, too many possibilities. The ESTPs need for freedom means that they may easily become stressed by situations or people who are inflexible. They dislike being tied down or controlled and may avoid marriage or even buying a house because of the fear of loss of freedom.

Much of the stress of ESTPs comes from using their less-preferred functions, Intuition and Feeling. Too many things to do or too many possibilities may lead to confusion for the ESTP and they may worry excessively about what is the right choice. ESTPs may be also be stressed by people whose behaviour is based more on emotion than logic or common sense. For example, they may be irritated by people who are upset about something but won't do anything about it, or people who are critical without knowing the facts of a situation.

Behaviour under stress
When stressed the ESTP may become rigid, argumentative or depressed, They will often focus on negative possibilities, expecting the worst to happen. If their inferior introverted Intuition takes over they may experience an unrealistic fear of what might go wrong or even have premonitions of negative things happening. In some cases they may have a sudden attraction to mystical or religious experience. They may withdraw and experience anxiety or depression, or they may express their anger and move on. The ESTP under stress will often lose spontaneity and feel unappreciated and bored. The boredom will often lead to laziness or disruptive behaviour.

If people do not deal with serious stress they may engage in unhealthy psychological games to reduce the effects of stress. An ESTP who is not coping with stress may resort to blackmail games such as tantrums or violent outbursts, risky behaviour that may be life-threatening, delinquency, boredom or serious depression. The unconscious reasons for this behaviour are to experience excitement and freedom, or to punish the person who has taken away their freedom. The long term effect of this behaviour is that they will often have their freedom taken away because of their behaviour.

How to reduce stress
The ESTP will often use physical activity, risk taking or new experiences, to reduce stress. They will usually seek the company of other people, preferring interaction to being alone. It is helpful for them to check the facts and be realistic about the situation, then use their internal logic to decide what is the appropriate action, before they act. To be healthy and to manage their stress it is essential that the ESTPs honour their basic need for freedom and action.

Leisure and Recreation
ESTPs are fun-loving and entertaining. They look for excitement and enjoy anything with an element of risk. They like to be actively involved or they quickly lose interest. ESTPs often enjoy the outdoors or activities that use up energy, many engaging in extreme sports like snow-boarding or parachuting. They may do some things alone such as motor-bike riding or horse riding, enjoying the sensing aspects of the experience. They often like music and dance. For ESTPs getting there is the fun part. Once there, like the Grand Canyon, "I've seen it now. Let's go".

ESTP often prefer action movies or adventure stories. They will tend to read about real things and situations e.g., history, technical areas that interest them, books about how things work or realistic stories that are descriptive.

ESTP Development

Childhood (6 - 12 years)
ESTP children are usually very active and interactive, and interested in everyone and everything. They are energetic, and fun-loving, and enjoy being the centre of attention. The Dominant function, extraverted Sensing, develops during this period so ESTP children are constantly active, interacting with people and things, and taking in vast amounts of information through their senses. They gather facts and details about reality. They want constant stimulation and become bored quickly if they don't have something to do. They will put a lot of energy into an activity until they lose interest. ESTPs interpret language and instructions literally, and trust what is real. They are humorous and like to be in the limelight.

The favourite activities for ESTP children usually focus on tangible and concrete activities. These often include sport; outdoor activities; collecting toys, rocks or football cards; assembling mechanical things, Lego or jigsaw puzzles; playing with computer games or transformer toys; playing practical jokes; performing. They prefer activity that has a purpose e.g. riding a horse to bring in the cattle. ESTPs often identify with sporting heroes or action figures like Spiderman or Bart Simpson.

Adolescence (13 - 20 years)
During adolescence the ESTP will spend more time reflecting and analysing internally as they develop their introverted Thinking. They will make their decisions using logic, but others may not understand their thought processes because they are internal. What others will observe is that ESTPs are honest and truthful and speak their mind. They need freedom and will resist control. They will respond positively to guidance from adults who understand them and encourage them to be themselves. They usually have a good social life but may find school frustrating because of the emphasis on theory rather than practical work. At this time the ESTP may appear shy and serious and may be reluctant to share their emotions.

Early Adulthood (20 - 35 years)
During this period the Third function, extraverted Feeling, emerges. This period may be confusing for ESTPs who have become comfortable with logical decision making and now are more sensitive to the feelings of others. They will focus more on values and relationships at this time, and will be more aware of what is important to them. Decisions will now be influenced by personal values as well as logic. ESTPs at this time will often become more tactful, sometimes sentimental and more easily hurt. Though they become more interested in personal relationships and intimacy at this time, they may still find it hard to get close to anyone.

Midlife (35 - 55 years)
At midlife ESTPs develop their introverted Intuition. The fun-loving interactive style of the ESTP continues, but now they will be more comfortable spending time alone reflecting. Their inner reflections are times of inspiration where they will focus on possibilities for the future and big picture concepts and theories. They will pay less attention to details and practical realities and may find themselves daydreamimg and forgetting things. They may begin to focus more on appreciating symbols and the meaning behind what is real. Some ESTPs may find exploring their inner intuitive world a little scary as it may lead them deep into the psyche. The creativity of ESTPs may increase at this time as they become more innovative. They will have their best inspirations when they are alone.

ENFP

Order of Functions:	Dominant	Ne
	Auxiliary	Fi
	Tertiary	Te
	Inferior	Si
Temperament:	Idealist (NF)	

Strengths

ENFPs are spontaneous, enthusiastic, optimistic, innovative and people-centred. They are idealistic. They value relationships and intimacy, and need to know that they are making a difference in the lives of people and in the world.

The Dominant gift of ENFPs is extraverted Intuition so they need a lot of interaction and enjoy new experiences. They scan the environment for ideas and connections and seek constant change. ENFPs work in bursts of inspiration and believe anything is possible. The supporting function of ENFPs is introverted Feeling, so they base important decisions on deep personal values. They like to have lots of people around to interact with and strive to help people reach their potential.

Potential difficulties

The less-preferred functions of the ENFP are extraverted Thinking and introverted Sensing. ENFPs are often restless and may act before thinking an idea through. They may find it difficult to assert themselves, wanting to avoid conflict and maintain harmony. Many ENFPs have difficulty with details and practical issues, and may not see reality. They often over-commit themselves and then have difficulty completing projects or meeting deadlines. They are not naturally organised so, if they lack discipline, they may not achieve what they want.

Communication

ENFP language tends to be global, positive, spontaneous and often humorous. Their extraverted Intuition sees connections in everything and wants to brainstorm ideas with others. They will often interrupt without meaning to because the ideas come so quickly. They talk freely about themselves, but only share the deeper feelings with people they are close to. Because their Feeling function is introverted they need time to reflect before they can talk about the important issues. ENFPs want affirmation for who they are. They expect honest and open communication and often have difficulty with people who are negative or closed-minded. If you want to change their ideas or behaviour explore the possibilities with them and show them how the change will benefit people.

Relationships

In a relationship ENFPs want intimacy and authenticity, as well as thoughtfulness and fun. Good relationships are the most important thing in the life of ENFPs so they try hard to make the relationship work. It is very important for them to be valued as they are and to be free to be themselves. ENFPs give a lot of praise and affection, and like to receive it. They constantly look for feedback, encouragement and support.

ENFPs are usually sensitive to other people's feelings and like to do things for the people they care about. They often intuit other people's feelings or needs and often put other people's needs first. Because their Feeling function is introverted it is difficult to express their deep feelings out loud, but they are very clear about what they value. They may need time to reflect before they can talk about how they feel. ENFPs avoid conflict until someone violates one of their deeper values.

Learning

ENFPs are imaginative and highly conceptual learners. They like complexity, theories and concepts, but need to be inspired to keep interested. They usually have very good language skills and often excel in subjects where they can express their ideas in verbal or written form. They usually find essay writing easy. They work in bursts of inspiration and love learning that stimulates the imagination. ENFPs use their extraverted Intuition to explore ideas and easily make connections. They often need to discuss ideas in order to understand, so they enjoy interactive group work. Their introverted Feeling focuses their interest on people and values.

ENFPs are usually keen readers and are attracted to learning in almost any area. They are often interested in language, history, fine arts, philosophy, psychology, music, astrology, metaphysics and healing. Some also do well in Science and Mathematics. ENFPs learn easily from books, group work, and project work, and thrive if they have the opportunity to be creative. In a classroom ENFPs lose interest quickly if the work is not challenging, if there is not enough interaction, or if their relationship with the teacher is not good. They often have difficulty meeting deadlines for assignments.

At Work

At work ENFPs want interaction, variety, flexibility and harmony. They love change and are constantly looking for new directions and new ways of doing things. They work in bursts of enthusiasm and need to be inspired to give their best. ENFPs have a lot of ideas and initiative, and like to have lots of things going on at the same time.

ENFPs need autonomy, to be free to follow their own path and to create change for people. They don't need a lot of structure or order because they have a clear structure in place on the inside. They like to work on projects that have boundaries, but can't bring closure until they are ready, so they may have difficulty with deadlines. ENFPs are nonconformists and will clash with authority if their values are violated.

Careers

ENFP's like to work helping people achieve their potential. They often choose careers in education, counselling, church ministry, healing, psychology, consulting and human resource management. Many ENFPs choose careers with opportunity for creative expression, such as journalism, advertising and marketing, and entertainment. ENFPs can be successful in any career if they value what they are doing.

Team Role

ENFPs are natural catalysts, creating change for others. They work well in teams where there is harmony, flexibility and support, and where they have autonomy. As team members they are flexible, energetic, creative and compassionate. Difficulties may arise if they don't meet deadlines, if they are too sensitive to criticism or if they don't deal with conflict.

Leadership Style

As leaders ENFPs often take on a mentoring role. They give direction, guidance and autonomy, allowing individuals to do things in their own way. ENFPs usually relate well to others, are supportive and enjoy facilitating teams. They like to work collaboratively. They are usually good communicators and, at their best, can be charismatic leaders.

The strengths of ENFPs are their ability to see all sides of an issue, to motivate others to create change and to get on well with people. Difficulties may occur if they spread their energy over too many projects, if they neglect the practical issues or if they do not assert themselves when necessary.

Stress for the ENFP

Causes of stress

ENFPs need to have meaningful relationships and to know that they are valued and are contributing to other people's lives. They will become stressed if they experience relationship problems or if they are unable to be themselves.

Since ENFPs prefer Intuition and Feeling much of their stress will come from using the less-preferred functions, Thinking and Sensing. ENFPs tend to take on too many things and may become stressed trying to meet deadlines or deal with practical things like filing and sorting, or facts and figures. ENFPs often have difficulty being assertive with people who are critical, inflexible, negative, controlling, or not open to change. They will often avoid confronting the problem until it becomes serious. ENFPs usually have difficulty being alone for long periods, preferring a lot of interaction.

Behaviour under stress

Introverted Sensing is usually the least developed function and the one most likely to get out of control under stress. ENFP under stress will often misplace things like car keys, or forget to do things or try to relieve the stress by going shopping. They may neglect their health and may become preoccupied with the situation replaying it over and over in their minds. If the inferior introverted Sensing takes over they may lose sight of the bigger picture and may become obsessive about insignificant facts and details. They may feel confused or overwhelmed or they may become preoccupied with their physical needs. Under serious stress they may withdraw in anger or become emotionally exhausted or depressed.

If people do not deal with stress they may engage in unhealthy psychological games to reduce the effects of stress. ENFPs who are not coping may ignore the symptoms or repress their feelings and delude themselves into thinking they are coping. The unconscious reason for this behaviour is to hide their feelings from others and themselves to avoid facing the issue. The long term effect of this behaviour is that it is difficult for them to have a really meaningful and honest relationship.

How to reduce stress

To reduce stress ENFPs will often engage in some kind of physical activity such as cleaning out cupboards. They often seek the company of other people to talk about the problem. Some ENFPs find it helpful to spend some quiet time relaxing or meditating. To be healthy and manage their stress it is essential that ENFPs honour their basic need for meaning and appreciation. They need to re-focus on the big picture and where they are making a difference in the world.

Leisure and Recreation

ENFPs enjoy a wide variety of leisure activities. They usually prefer activities where they can interact with people. And they enjoy learning something that will help people or will help them understand people. Their interests may include things like art, music, singing, drama, surfing, astrology, metaphysics, travel, healing, parties, dinner with friends, weekend workshops or sport. They often feel a strong connection with the ocean. Some ENFPs have an interest in a very specific area such as the Russian Royal Family, World War II Aviation, or British dance music of the 1930s. They will usually only share this with someone who shows an interest.

ENFP reading will focus on the imagination and possibilities for people and humanity. This may include classic romance novels like *Pride and Prejudice*, history, fantasy, spirituality, healing, travel, self-help books and new age topics. ENFPs don't necessarily read a book from beginning to end, but will often read the sections that interest them first.

ENFP Development

Childhood (6 - 12 years)

ENFP children are enthusiastic, imaginative, sensitive and caring children who seek constant interaction. The Dominant function, extraverted Intuition, develops during childhood so they spend a lot of time with others in activities that engage the imagination. They particularly enjoy activities that are new and creative. ENFP children can find an endless variety of creative things to do, such as art, music, dance, drama and reading stories about people or magical places, dressing up, role playing and daydreaming about the future. Many ENFP children will sing or perform in front of their friends or on stage. They usually make friends easily and dislike conflict amongst their friends or family.

Although ENFPs usually enjoy reading at this age they are often very busy and may not spend much time reading. ENFPs usually have difficulty paying attention to practical tasks and are easily bored with routine or silence. They may engage in sport or practical games, but will often find themselves daydreaming in the midst of it. They enjoy being creative but need constant interaction with others.

Adolescence (13 - 20 years)

During adolescence the ENFP will spend time reflecting and considering the things they value, as they develop their introverted Feeling. They will spend time reflecting on how they could contribute to making the world a better place. They will often read books on psychology, self-help or spirituality. They will make their decisions using personal values, but others may not understand the depth of their inner values. At this time ENFPs may appear shy and may find it difficult to assert themselves. What others will observe is that they are honest and sensitive to the pain of others. ENFPs need the freedom to be themselves and will resist control, and may rebel. They respond positively to guidance from adults who understand them and encourage them to be themselves. ENFPs have a good social life and usually do well at school.

Early Adulthood (20 - 35 years)

During this period the Third function, extraverted Thinking, emerges. The fun-loving personality of the ENFP continues throughout adulthood but, as the Thinking emerges, the ENFP will become more assertive, more logical in making decisions and less concerned about offending others. They may even appear aggressive as they begin to take charge of their own lives and feel a greater sense of freedom to be themselves. Some ENFPs at this time will look for new challenges in work or in the academic field. They may find themselves setting up business ventures or beginning study in psychology, business or management. They will be more confident in expressing their opinion and in making decisions.

Midlife (35 - 55 years)

During this period the Fourth function, introverted Sensing, develops. The outgoing, idealistic personality of the ENFP will continue throughout adulthood, but now their attention turns to the inner world of reality, facts, details and sensory experience. They will seek more quiet time and will focus more on their health issues and on practical activities. Many ENFPs at this time will become involved in activities such as art, craft, massage, meditation, natural healing, gardening, housework, sport or dancing. Some ENFPs become interested in writing to share what they have learned about life with others. Some become advocates for disadvantaged people. ENFPs at midlife will be more comfortable living with reality and will often find they enjoy their own company.

ENTP

Order of Functions:	Dominant	Ne
	Auxiliary	Ti
	Tertiary	Fe
	Inferior	Si
Temperament:	Rational (NT)	

Strengths

ENTPs are spontaneous, energetic and innovative lateral thinkers. They value knowledge and competence, and need autonomy and intellectual freedom.

The Dominant gift of ENTPs is extraverted Intuition so they enjoy a lot of interaction, new experiences and creating new solutions. They scan the environment for ideas and connections, and seek constant change. ENTPs work in bursts of inspiration. The supporting function of the ENTP is introverted Thinking, so they base important decisions on internal logic. They like complex problems and construct internal models to find solutions. ENTPs are constantly questioning and seeking ways to improve whatever they are involved in.

Potential difficulties

The less-preferred functions of the ENTP are extraverted Feeling and introverted Sensing. ENTPs are not always aware of people's feelings and may unintentionally say things that offend others. Their high expectations may lead them to be over-critical. ENTPs lose interest in projects when they become bored and struggle to complete what they start. They are often impatient. They may make spontaneous decisions that create great change before they have thought it through. Many ENTPs forget details and often lose things.

Communication

ENTP communication is usually direct, logical, inventive, spontaneous and humorous. Their extraverted Intuition enjoys brainstorming ideas and sharing what they know. Their internal logic likes to question, sometimes mischievously e.g., "Why is Abbreviation such a long word?" and "Why isn't the word Phonetic spelled the way it sounds ?" They love to debate and can be very convincing even when they are wrong. They need intellectual freedom, to think their own thoughts, and can summarise a long a complex conversation in one sentence. ENTPs expect honest and open communication and may have difficulty with someone who is emotional or closed-minded. They may find it hard to share their feelings. Their language tends to be global, impersonal and logical. If you want to change their ideas or behaviour give them logical reasons and be prepared to discuss and debate the issues.

Relationships

In relationships ENTPs want humour, thoughtfulness and intellectual conversation. They also like the unusual and the unexpected. They like to share a common goal, but also need autonomy. As partners ENTPs are often strong, loving and outrageous. Their way of caring is based more on treating people fairly rather than kindly. Feelings are important to them, but not always highest priority. So, ENTPs may not display a lot of affection and may forget to say "Thankyou".

ENTPs want to be respected as competent in a relationship, so they will analyse people to work out how to behave around them. As their extraverted Feeling develops in early adulthood they will feel more compassion for others and be more comfortable showing physical affection.

Learning

ENTPs are life-long learners with an insatiable appetite for knowledge and competence. They are highly conceptual, self-directed learners and lateral thinkers. They work in bursts of inspiration, easily make connections and love problem solving. ENTPs use their extraverted Intuition to explore ideas and see connections. They need to discuss and criticise ideas in order to understand, so they enjoy debating issues, often from both sides. Their introverted Thinking develops during adolescence and enables them to logically evaluate information quickly, according to an internal model. Because their Thinking is introverted they may find it hard to explain in words how or why they arrived at a particular conclusion.

ENTPs usually read continuously on almost any topic of a theoretical nature. Their interests are varied and they are often attracted to learning in areas such as engineering, law, science, music, art, information technology, languages, and more. They learn easily from books, group work, internet and debates, and thrive if they have opportunities to be creative. In a classsroom ENTPs become bored very quickly if the work is not intellectually challenging, if there is not enough interaction, or if the teacher is not competent. If they lose interest they sometimes become disruptive.

At Work

At work ENTPs want a interaction, variety, flexibility and fun. They love change and innovation, constantly reinventing, their job, themselves and the organisation. ENTPs are continually learning and applying new theories to their organisation. Once they have mastered something they will get bored and move on. ENTPs work in bursts of activity and need autonomy, to be free to work in their own way to make things happen.

ENTPs need problems to solve and opportunities to show their competence. They can see many options in a situation and need to interact to explore their ideas with others. They are non-conformists who often challenge existing ideas and accepted practices. They may clash with authority if they don't respect the leader or the rules. ENTPs may have difficulty completing projects on time and often speak before thinking.

Careers

ENTPs want opportunities to create change and learn something new. They will change their career when it ceases to be a challenge. ENTPs often work in industrial relations, change management, human resource development, strategic planning, computers, sales, teaching, marketing and advertising and career development. One ENTP may try all of these.

Team Role

ENTPs are natural change agents and motivators. They work well in teams that have short-term goals and can get immediate results. They need the opprotunity to show their competence and solve problems, and usually need people on the team who can attend to the details. Difficulties may arise if they ignore people's feelings or if they don't meet deadlines.

Leadership Style

ENTPs are active managers who take on a mentoring role, giving direction and guidance. They encourage autonomy, allowing individuals to do things in their own way. ENTPs enjoy facilitating teams to work through an issue. They give accurate feedback, and can be supportive and tough, but fair. If a person is not performing, they will insist on improvement.

The strengths of ENTPs are their high energy level, and their ability to see all sides of a situation and to motivate others to create change. Difficulties occur if they spread their energy over too many projects, if they neglect the practical issues or if they are not sensitive to other people's feelings.

Stress for the ENTP

Causes of stress
ENTPs have a basic need for competence and intellectual freedom, and will experience stress if they lose their autonomy or if they experience incompetence in themselves or others. They are stressed by people with closed minds and situations where they can see a solution but are told not to execute it.

Since ENTPs prefer Intuition and Thinking much of their stress will come from using the less-preferred functions, Feeling and Sensing. Introverted Sensing is usually the least developed function and the one most likely to get out of control under stress. ENTPs tend to take on too many things and may become stressed trying to meet deadlines or deal with practical things like filing and sorting, or facts and figures. ENTPs often have difficulty dealing with strong emotions and are stressed by people who are controlling or not logical, or who judge them unfairly. They are usually irritated by office politics and small talk and may be stressed by being alone for long periods.

Behaviour under stress
When stressed ENTPs will often misplace things like car keys or may forget to do things. They may neglect their health and become preoccupied with a situaion analysing it over and over. They may become very focused on the task, making lists and prioritising, or they may withdraw. If the inferior introverted Sensing takes over they may lose sight of the big picture and the possibilities. They may become preoccupied with their physical needs. They may also become angry and irrational, criticising others or playing practical jokes that are hurtful.

If people do not deal with serious stress they may engage in unhealthy psychological games to reduce the effects of the stress. ENTPs who are not coping with stress may shut out all emotions, dismissing them as irrelevant. They may also avoid situations where they feel incompetent. The unconscious reasons for this behaviour are to regain the feeling of being in control and being competent, and to appear competent to others. The long term effect of this behaviour is that a fear of failure will inhibit learning and lead to incompetence.

How to reduce stress
ENTPs will often use physical activity such as running or working out in a gym to reduce stress. They usually seek the company of other people preferring interaction to being alone. They may find it helpful to reduce the amount of activity and spend some time setting priorities and talking about it with someone. They need to focus on the big picture and recognise their achievements. To be healthy and manage their stress it is essential that ENTPs honour their basic need for competence.

Leisure and Recreation
ENTPs love doing things that are unusual and challenging and like to win awards at national or international level. They enjoy travel, preferring a new culture where they can learn a new language. They like films that make them think and will analyse the action and cinematography. They often like drama, seeing the people in a play as actors practising their craft, rather than as people. They like word games and strategic games like chess. Other leisure activities could include sport, outdoor activities like bushwalking, tri-athlon or canoeing, painting, or cooking dinner for friends. They like humour, particularly Monty Python, Farside or black humour.

ENTP reading includes novels, magazines, detective stories, newspapers, business and systems thinking e.g., *Approaching the Corporate Heart* or *Chaos and Complexity Theory* . ENTPs often skim books or read summaries. ENTPs reading novels are more interested in analysing the use of language or the plot construction, than character development.

ENTP Development

Childhood (6 - 12 years)
ENTPs are energetic, gregarious, imaginative, independent children who seek constant interaction. During childhood the Dominant function, extraverted Intuition, develops so they spend a lot of time with others in activities that engage the imagination. They particularly enjoy activities that are new and creative. This may include reading books or telling convincing imaginary stories of great adventures they have had, like playing with tigers in India. Many ENTP children sing or perform in front of their friends or on stage. They usually make friends easily but may not bond well with them. ENTP children are independent thinkers with a strong sense of justice. They will clash with authority if they believe their rights are not respected or their teachers are incompetent.

ENTPs have enquiring minds and often read widely to gain useful information they can apply. For example, one ENTP read every book in the local library on surveying and then surveyed the back yard using surveyor's pegs. ENTPs may also enjoy playing chess, sport or music, or playing with animals. They will engage in many different kinds of activities and will strive to achieve recognition for their competence. They could easily achieve the award for the "Best All-Rounder".

Adolescence (13 - 20 years)
During adolescence ENTPs develop introverted Thinking and their search for independence becomes obvious as they analyse and question everything. They often argue with their parents on matters of principle. Some will openly challenge the education system if it is too rigid or if they see it as not catering for student needs. Other people may see ENTPs as radical or anarchists. In fact, they are independent thinkers developing their internal logic. They need intellectual freedom and will resist control. They respond positively to guidance from adults they respect as competent. Although they want some quiet time during adolescence ENTPs still need to interact and usually have an active social life. They may not be sensitive to the feelings of others and may appear to be more interested in winning a debate than getting on with people.

Early Adulthood (20 - 35 years)
During this period the Third function, extraverted Feeling, emerges. This period may be confusing for ENTPs who have become comfortable with logical decision making and are now more sensitive to the feelings of others. They will often become more tactful, sometimes sentimental and more easily hurt. Some may experience turbulent emotions or feel teary when they talk about things that are important to them. Though they are now more interested in relationships and intimacy they may still feel disconnected from people. Some ENTPs will turn to books or study to find answers, taking courses in psychotherapy, child psychology or relationships.

Midlife (35 - 55 years)
During this period the Fourth function, introverted Sensing, develops. The outgoing and logical personality of the ENTPs continues in adulthood, but now their attention turns to the inner world of reality, facts, details and sensory experience. They will focus more on things other than the mind, such as health and physical fitness, possibly going to the gym or learning massage, taking up a sport or an outdoor activity such as gardening. ENTPs at midlife will often seek more quiet time and may take up meditation or may spend time just sitting and relaxing. They may become fascinated by useless trivia, like Top 10 lists. Many ENTPs will become more comfortable with reality and may keep their homes much tidier.

ENFJ

Order of Functions:	Dominant	Fe
	Auxiliary	Ni
	Tertiary	Se
	Inferior	Ti
Temperament:	Idealist (NF)	

Strengths

ENFJs are energetic, sociable, imaginative and idealistic. They like having people around and thrive on helping people to develop. They want to make a difference in the world, as well as making sure they become all they can be.

The Dominant gift of ENFJs is extraverted Feeling, so they need to connect with people and see this contact as more important than rules or plans. They want to create harmony in the world and will fight to protect the rights of others. The supporting function of ENFJs is introverted Intuition, so they see what is possible in the future and quickly generate new ideas. They usually enjoy symbols, stories, myths and dreams.

Potential difficulties

The less-preferred functions of the ENFJs are extraverted Sensing and introverted Thinking, so they may not deal well with reality or details, and may have difficulty connecting ideas logically. Sometimes ENFJs are oversensitive and may see problems that aren't there. They may try too hard to please others or win approval. They often have difficulty saying 'No' and give too much time and energy to other people, and then become exhausted.

Communication

ENFJs are enthusiastic communicators. Their language tends to be focused on feelings and concepts. They are strategic, working out the best mode of communication with a person to get their message across. In conversations they tend to share personal stories or use analogies, rather than give details or facts. They read body language and look for congruence in the language, behaviour and body language. ENFJs enjoy any opportunity to communicate, with the local shopkeeper, with friends over coffee, or waiting for email messages. They sometimes get emotional when talking about themselves and feel vulnerable, so they will only share personal stories with people they trust. If you want to change their ideas or their behaviour appeal to their values. Explain tactfully that their behaviour is disregarding the feelings or rights of others.

Relationships

ENFJs are sociable and usually relate easily to people. They want to make an authentic connection to other people, to be able to be themselves and know that they are accepted and supported by the other. They don't relate to people who are critical, intolerant or unsupportive. They can usually sense at the first meeting if a person is trustworthy. Trust is important to ENFJs. They tend to trust people implicitly, believing that everyone is good. So, when that trust is broken, they will feel betrayed. They may forgive, but will never trust you again.

ENFJs are devoted to their families and see them as their source of strength. They easily make friends with people if they respect their values. They are natural romantics, often looking for the perfect relationship. They enjoy being in love. The Feeling function of ENFJs is extraverted so they like to maintain harmony and avoid confrontation. They are very nurturing, supportive and sensitive to people's needs. They enjoy giving gifts to those they care about.

Learning

ENFJs are imaginative, conceptual learners who learn best in a supportive interactive environment. Their Intuition is introverted, so they enjoy abstract concepts and theories that relate to people. They are constantly trying to see patterns and look for the meaning behind the words. Once they have the big picture they may lose interest in the details. They are usually keen readers with very good language skills. ENFJs are organised and like to finish everything. They work best if they are inspired, easily see connections and enjoy learning that stimulates the imagination and focuses on people.

ENFJs strive for excellence and usually do well academically. They are often attracted to learning in areas such as history, anthropology, mythology, music, languages, psychology, art, poetry and other forms of writing. They thrive in classes where there is harmony and cooperation, and the opportunity to be creative. ENFJs will lose interest in learning if it does not stimulate the imagination or if there is no personal support.

At Work

ENFJs need a work environment that is congruent with their personal, emotional and spiritual values. They will often bring nature scenes, photographs and music into their workspace. They enjoy facilitating people and their development, and believe that people are the organisations greatest asset. When managing tasks with specific outcomes they will focus on the people, knowing that the outcomes will be achieved. They like to know that they have made a difference.

ENFJs have a strong desire for harmony, but will confront issues and stand up against injustice. They are organised and conscientious and value personal integrity more than any financial reward. They may have difficulty with details and may exhaust themselves if they take on too much.

Careers

ENFJs need to work with people, and they particularly enjoy working with people who are struggling to find solutions to their problems. They often take on the role of a teacher or therapist and are thrilled when the person they are working with achieves success. Common careers for ENFJs are outplacement counselling, training, music, church ministry, psychology, child development, counselling, journalism, public speaking, nursing, art, coaching and medicine.

Team Role

ENFJs love working in teams. They understand people and communicate easily, providing inspiration and support. They trust other team members and harmonize the team. ENFJs need autonomy and closure and will ensure that projects are completed on time. Difficulties may arise if they take on too much work, if they lose sight of reality, or if they miss the details and draw the wrong conclusions.

Leadership Style

ENFJs are enthusiastic and supportive leaders who usually inspire their team. They are not authoritarian, preferring to allow team members some autonomy. They often take on a mentoring role in a team, and can motivate people to want to achieve and work together. They focus on creating harmony in the team and provide the support necessary for individuals to develop. ENFJs are protective of their team and generous with rewards.

The strengths of ENFJs include their ability to facilitate the development of individual potential, their personal integrity, and the ability to vision the future. Difficulties may occur if there is a conflict of values, if they neglect the practical needs of the organisation, or if they do not assert themselves.

Stress for the ENFJ

Causes of stress
ENFJs need to have meaningful harmonious relationships and know that they are contributing to people's lives. They will be stressed by conflict, especially face to face, and also by lack of harmony, loss of control, a conflict of values, being alone for too long or too much sensory stimulation.

Since ENFJs prefer Feeling and Intuition, much of their stress is likely to come from using their less-preferred functions, Sensing and Thinking. ENFJs often have difficulty asserting themselves and are sensitive to criticism from others. They may be irritated by people who are intolerant, prejudiced or critical. They are often stressed by routine, details, repetition, missing deadlines, and practical things like too much clutter.

Behaviour under stress
Introverted Thinking is usually the least developed function of the ENFJ and the one most likely to get out of control under stress. When very stressed ENFJs may become impersonal, cold and inflexible. They may explode and say harsh or cruel things to people, and feel guilty about it later. If they are hurt or criticised ENFJs may become quiet and keep their feelings to themselves. They may find it difficult to maintain order and may have chronic insomnia, lying awake at night planning the next day in detail. When stressed they use a lot of emotional energy and become tired. In extreme cases they may shut down and even dissociate from their bodies. ENFJs will often battle with the stress on their own rather than ask for help.

If people do not deal with stress they may engage in unhealthy psychological games to reduce the effects of the stress. ENFJs who are not coping may ignore the symptoms or repress their feelings. They may delude themselves into thinking they are being true to themselves. The unconscious reason for this behaviour is to hide their feelings of not being genuine. The long term effect of this behaviour is that they will find it difficult to enter into a really meaningful and honest relationship.

How to reduce stress
To reduce stress ENFJs often use meditation or read self-help books, looking for clarity and inspiration. They may find that music or contact with nature or people is helpful. To be healthy and manage their stress it is essential that ENFJs honour their basic need for meaning and a sense of identity. It is often helpful to re-focus on the big picture and where they are making a difference in the world.

Leisure and Recreation
ENFJs often enjoy a balance of social and reflective leisure activities. They need to connect with people, and to use the imagination. Some favourite activities include weekends away, dinner parties, bush walking, team sports, movies, swimming or going to the beach. ENFJs like movies and books about movies, and enjoy seeing how the book is translated onto the screen. They go to a movie to be moved. The images in story and film help them to make sense of their extraverted Feeling function. ENFJs enjoy beautiful things like roses, sunsets, music, paintings, water and the bush. These stimulate their Intuition and may inspire them to write poetry. ENFJs enjoy listening to music, rarely paying attention to the words unless they are about relationships. They often like quiet activities like reading, meditation, yoga, visualisation and fantasy.

ENFJs usually read self-help books, mysteries with clues to solve, spirituality books, poetry and classic literature such as novels by Jane Austin, or the Bronte sisters, or the English classics. They don't usually like science fiction. For humour they often enjoy a play on words.

ENFJ Development

Childhood (6 - 12 years)
ENFJ children are enthusiastic, imaginative, talkative and caring. During childhood their Dominant function, extraverted Feeling develops, so ENFJs are naturally outgoing. They need to care for and interact with people. They often bubble with enthusiasm and introduce themselves to strangers. They enjoy helping people and looking after children and animals, and at school will sit next to someone who is lonely. ENFJs are often leaders amongst their friends, organising the other children to play or perform together. They enjoy caring and sharing and are sometimes show-offs. They are cooperative children, eager to please. They need harmony and approval and will often withdraw if there is conflict.

ENFJ children usually enjoy singing, dancing, art, talking, fairy stories, sandplay, make-believe play, speaking to groups and may have imaginary playmates. Their favourite playthings are often art and craft materials and teddy bears that they can cuddle. They enjoy reading, writing and hearing stories

Adolescence (13 - 20 years)
During adolescence ENFJs develop introverted Intuition so they have a rich imaginary life with dreams of romance, far away places and how they can help people in need. Some become interested in mythology or literature, or may read or write poetry. Many develop an interest in their spiritual life and make decisions to do something worthwhile with their lives. At school they mix with many groups of children, often gravitating towards the leaders. They are protective of other children. They may even find themselves protesting against rules or unjust political structures. ENFJs spend a lot of time at parties, dances, drama groups and youth groups, often as the organiser. They need autonomy and usually do well academically. They respond positively to guidance from adults who understand them and encourage them to be themselves.

Early Adulthood (20 - 35 years)
During this period the extraverted Sensing, develops. Now ENFJs turn their attention to the outer world of reality, facts, details and sensory experience. They will be more observant of details in nature and may engage in activities that stimulate the senses, the sights, sounds, smells. Some will engage in physical exercise and outdoor walks, even trekking in Nepal, and enjoying the sensory experience. They may take up new practical activities like baking, knitting complicated patterns or medieval tapestry, often inventing their own designs or different ways of stitching. Sometimes these activities will stimulate them to write poetry. ENFJs will often become more comfortable living in the present and dealing with reality and will enjoy creating harmonious physical environments. At this age many ENFJs will choose to work in helping professions where they can make a real difference in people's lives.

Midlife (35 - 55 years)
During Midlife the Fourth function, introverted Thinking, emerges. ENFJs spend a lot of time thinking things through, analysing situations and making more logical decisions as they become more independent. Now they can logically justify decisions that were previously based on 'gut feelings'. They also become aware of the tension between maintaining the harmony and following their own beliefs and ideals. The outgoing, caring personality of the ENFJ continues but, as the Thinking emerges, they will have a strong desire to assert themselves and may become confrontational. They are less concerned about offending others as they begin to take charge of their own lives and feel a greater freedom to be themselves.

ESFJ

Order of Functions:	Dominant	Fe
	Auxiliary	Si
	Tertiary	Ne
	Inferior	Ti
Temperament:	Guardian (SJ)	

Strengths

ESFJs are caring, practical, busy people who relate well to others. They need to interact with people and value their contribution to building up a caring, supportive community. They value traditions and are very loyal to friends and family.

The Dominant gift of ESFJs is extraverted Feeling so they need to connect with people and love to organise them. They love schedules, calendars and lists. They love pleasing people and creating harmony, and find it difficult to say "No". The supporting function of ESFJs is introverted Sensing, so they are practical and realistic, and able to deal with facts and details. They trust what they know from experience and have a great capacity for recalling sensory details from past.

Potential difficulties

ESFJs find it difficult to function without harmony and support. The less-preferred functions of ESFJs are extraverted Intuition and introverted Thinking, so they usually find it difficult to deal with conflict and may withdraw rather than assert themselves. They may try too hard to please others or win their approval. They may difficulty saying 'No' and give too much time and energy to other people. They are sometimes impatient and may act before they think. Many ESFJs find it difficult to visualise what is possible in the future.

Communication

ESFJs are enthusiastic communicators. Their language tends to focus on feelings and facts about people. They often think out loud and say things before they realise what they have said. They like to know a lot of details, so they ask a lot of questions. ESFJs like clear and specific instructions. They tend to interpret language literally and may have difficulty with symbols and metaphors. They thrive on affirmation. ESFJs enjoy talking, and want closure when they discuss something. They often use pictures, colours, or touch to communicate. For example, hearts on their bracelets are not symbols but are statements about the importance of love in their lives. If you want to change their ideas or their behaviour explain why it matters and the affect it's having, and show that you care.

Relationships

ESFJs are sociable and relate easily to people. They usually have many friends, and often have close friends they have known since childhood. They want people to be comfortable and will talk to anyone who is left out. ESFJs need affection, honesty and security in personal relationships. They put a lot of energy into friendships and love pleasing people they care about. They don't relate to people who are critical and feel enormous disappointment if a friend lets them down.

Family is very important to ESFJs. They value photographs and keepsakes that remind them of the past. They like to create a warm atmosphere at home with lighting, candles and colour. They need friends and family to make contact on special occasions. The Feeling function of ESFJs focuses on maintaining harmony, so they may avoid confrontation. They are nurturing, supportive and sensitive to people's needs.

Learning

ESFJs learn through experience and interaction, and learn best in an environment that is supportive, neat and tidy. They have a good memory for facts, especially facts about people. They perceive mainly through their senses and so need the sensory or practical experience before they are given the theory. They fit well into the school system because they are cooperative and love rules, structure, timetables and uniforms.

ESFJs are conscientious students who willingly do homework and practise to improve their skills. They like learning that is clear and measurable, such as modern history, economics, home economics, music, mathematics, speech, drama, dance and sport. They will thrive in classes where there is harmony, interaction and hands-on learning. ESFJs will lose interest if the learning is not relevant to real life, or if there is a lack of personal support. They may struggle to achieve academically if the teaching is too theoretical or the instructions are not specific enough.

At Work

ESFJs are hard-working and need structure, interaction and harmony in the workplace. They care for the people they work with and want to help them develop, but they are also very committed to getting the job done. They are organised, tidy and reliable and will persist until the work is completed. They will only work for a company if they believe in what it is doing, so they are able give great loyalty to the company.

ESFJs like their work environment to be comfortable. They often bring to work things that represent relationships or make their surroundings more comfortable, such as stuffed toys, Thankyou cards, fragrant oil burners or their children's pictures. ESFJs are often stressed by office politics and, if they feel powerless to change things they will leave.

Careers

ESFJs need to work with people and enjoy helping them to achieve and develop. They often take on the role of teacher or trainer and can create an harmonious environment that is conducive to openness and sharing. Common careers for ESFJs include human resource development, training, school teaching, vocational education, hairdresser, administration, banking, nursing, radio announcer and hospitality.

Team Role

ESFJs love working in teams and enjoy facilitating group work. They are in touch with the needs of others and take a personal interest in team members, often keeping contact after they leave the organisation. They create harmony, attend to the practical details and ensure projects are completed on time. Difficulties may arise if they take on too much work, if they overpower others, or if there are no clear plans or outcomes.

Leadership Style

ESFJs are diplomatic and supportive leaders. They are able to organise others to complete tasks on time and ensure that the practical issues are taken care of. As leaders they often take on a teaching or a mentoring role, helping people achieve and work together cooperatively. They focus on the people, creating harmony and providing the support necessary for each individual to develop. ESFJs are protective of their team and generous with affirmation. They create stability and provide clear work plans, procedures and definite outcomes.

The strengths of ESFJs include their organising ability, their attention to detail and their support of their staff. Difficulties may occur if they avoid conflict and do not assert themselves when necessary, if they don't allow others enough autonomy or if they take on too much and forget to delegate.

Stress for the ESFJ

Causes of stress
ESFJs need interaction with people in a supportive family or group and will often be stressed by disharmony or lack of support, or being alone for too long. They are sensitive to criticism and find conflict stressful, especially face to face. ESFJs will be stressed by loss of control or indecision.

Since ESFJs prefer Feeling and Sensing, much of their stress comes from using the less-preferreded functions, Intuition and Thinking. They may be stressed by lack of detail, lack of clear guidelines or too many possibilities. They often have difficulty being assertive and may be stressed when logical reasons or explanations are demanded of them or by people who are unjust or critical. They are stressed by office politics and by people who lack commitment or don't keep their word.

Behaviour under stress
Introverted Thinking and Extraverted Intuition are usually the least developed functions of the ESFJ and the ones most likely to get out of control under stress. When stressed ESFJs will often worry constantly about what might go wrong, the negative possibilities. They may have negative thoughts about themselves which lead to depression. They may complain a lot, or let the feelings smoulder and say nothing. Under great stress they may lose their temper and shout. If they are hurt or criticised ESFJs will often try to turn the other person around, but if that doesn't work, they will walk away. If stressed by too much to do the ESFJ will usually just work until it is done.

If people don't deal with stress they may engage in unhealthy psychological games to reduce the effects of stress. ESFJs who are not coping with stress may nag or become depressed, or they may become overprotective and critical of those close to them. The unconscious reason for this behaviour is to manipulate others into giving them attention so they feel a sense of belonging. The long term effect is that this behaviour drives people away and they lose their sense of belonging.

How to reduce stress
To reduce stress ESFJs often relax having dinner with friends or at a night club or pub. They will often engage in physical activity such as gym or exercise classes, boxing, walking with a friend, gardening or simply smelling the roses. They like to talk about the situation to a friend or work colleague. ESFJs may find that music, or contact with nature or people is helpful. To be healthy and manage their stress it is essential that ESFJs honour their basic needs for structure and belonging.

Leisure and Recreation
ESFJs usually enjoy a busy social life. While they need to connect with people, they also enjoy doing physical activity. Some favourite activities with friends and family may include dinner parties, weekends away, barbecues, picnics, parties, movies with happy endings, walking, cycling, tennis, travel, watching or playing sport, swimming, fishing and going to the beach. ESFJs also enjoy some activities without interaction, such as gardening, cooking, listening to or playing music, word games, reading, time with their animals or meditation. ESFJs usually complete their work first so they can look forward to the play. They plan holidays in advance and usually celebrate special events in a traditional way. They give a lot of attention to organising and preparing social events so that all of the details are attended to and the guests are well looked after.

ESFJs usually read books that are people-focused, such as autobiographies or books with life messages like *The Art of Happiness* and *The Velveteen Rabbit*. They often enjoy the classic novel by authors like Charles Dickens, and may enjoy books on gardening and travel.

ESFJ Development

Childhood (6 - 12 years)
ESFJ children are talkative, realistic, caring and eager to please. During childhood their Dominant function, extraverted Feeling, develops so ESFJ children are outgoing and need to care for and interact with people. They enjoy helping people, looking after children and animals, and visiting people in a hospital. ESFJ children like to organise people and often want to be in control. They may be seen as bossy and sometimes enjoy showing off. They need harmony and approval and will withdraw if there is conflict. ESFJs like to organise their belongings and keep everything in its right place. Books are often organised in alphabetical order.

ESFJ children usually enjoy singing, dancing, music, school musicals, craft, sport, athletics, cooking, helping their parents at home, climbing trees or organising concerts with the neighbourhood children. They often keep their favourite toy well into adulthood. They usually enjoy reading books about real life stories or facts more than fantasy.

Adolescence (13 - 20 years)
During adolescence ESFJs develop introverted Sensing, so they usually enjoy doing practical and tangible things for people or doing physical activity like hockey, basketball, athletics, tennis, tap dancing, jazz ballet, drama or playing a musical instrument. They often receive good-citizenship awards, or are selected as class captain or class prefect. ESFJs take these responsibilities very seriously and will ensure that the other children follow the rules, even if the rules don't make much sense to the ESFJ. During this time ESFJs often become a little more reflective than in childhood and may be content with one or two friends. They organise their schoolwork and study time to complete work on time. Their need to connect with people continues, so ESFJs generally have a good social life during this time but many of their activities will focus on family.

Early Adulthood (20 - 35 years)
During this period the Third function, extraverted Intuition, develops. Now ESFJs will focus more on the possibilities for the future. They will enjoy discussions and brainstorming more than before and easily see links and connections. They may begin to miss details and become forgetful and absent-minded as their imagination becomes more active. ESFJs at this age are usually very busy and may not spend much time reflecting until they approach midlife. They often join sporting or social groups and may volunteer to work in community service organisations such as Lifeline. ESFJs may also experience an increase in creativity at this time. They may have new inspirations and hunches and may spend time daydreaming and looking towards the future.

Midlife (35 - 55 years)
During Midlife the Fourth function, introverted Thinking, emerges. ESFJs will spend a lot of time thinking things through, analysing situations and making more logical decisions as they become more independent. Now they can recognise that some decisions need to be logical and will usually not be so fearful of the conflict that may result. Now they are able to give clear instructions with logical reasons and give objective feedback. The outgoing and caring personality of the ESFJ continues but, as the Thinking emerges, they will have a strong desire to assert themselves and become confrontational when necessary. They will become less concerned about offending others as they begin to take charge of their own lives and feel a greater sense of freedom to be themselves.

ENTJ

Order of Functions:	Dominant	Te
	Auxiliary	Ni
	Tertiary	Se
	Inferior	Fi
Temperament:	Rational (NT)	

Strengths

ENTJs are outgoing, visionary, systematic and independent people who can achieve anything if the goal is clear and they are motivated. They are competitive and self-determined, and they thrive on solving complex problems.

The Dominant function of ENTJs is extraverted Thinking so they tend to base their decisions on logic. ENTJs are task-focused and like order, structure and autonomy. They love to organise and are natural strategic planners. They value fairness and equity. The supporting function of ENTJs is their introverted Intuition, so they see patterns and connections and want the framework first and details later. They use intuition to find solutions and often know things before they happen.

Potential difficulties

ENTJs find it difficult to function if there is a lack of organisation, if goals are unclear, or if they work for too long on their own. Their less-preferred functions are extraverted Sensing and introverted Feeling, so they are not always sensitive to the impact of their decisions on people, and can have difficulty understanding people. At times they may be inflexible and critical. They may have difficulty with details and practical issues and may not always have facts to support their views.

Communication

ENTJs are enthusiastic communicators. Being intuitive their language tends to be global, dealing with concepts and ideas. When they are very excited they may not finish their sentences. Their Thinking function is extraverted so they explain things logically and challenge other people's ideas hoping to improve on them. ENTJs need intellectual freedom, the freedom to think and speak their own thoughts. They are direct and outspoken. They expect honest and open communication and may have difficulty with someone who is emotional or closed-minded. In discussions they want closure and solutions, rather than open-ended exploration. They rarely talk about emotions, especially in the workplace. If you want to change their ideas or behaviour, state your goals up front, give logical reasons and be prepared to discuss and debate the issues.

Relationships

ENTJs make lots of friends but are close to only a few. They put a lot of effort into their relationships, which other people may not recognise. They feel things deeply but do not want to discuss them or explore them because the feelings are overwhelming. They need to feel competent in relationships.

ENTJs find it easy to separate work and family life. At work they tend to use the Thinking function to deal with people, and would consider outbursts of emotion as unprofessional. At home they are more comfortable with feelings and values and are affectionate with those they are close to. ENTJs are not usually comfortable with a lot of affection, believing that actions speak louder than words. If they are betrayed or hurt in a relationship they will often feel shattered or powerless. They encourage independence in their children and are very consistent in how they relate to them.

Learning

ENTJs are imaginative, conceptual learners who learn best in a challenging and interactive environment. The combination of Intuition and logic leads them to enjoy dealing with abstract concepts, theories and strategic thinking. They value learning for its own sake and like to solve complex problems. They are not usually interested in the details but often want to apply the learning in the external world. They are usually keen readers with very good language skills. They are organised and like to finish everything.

ENTJs are high achievers who strive for excellence and do well academically. From an early age they often receive awards for achievement. They are often attracted to learning in areas such as science, anthropology, palaeontology, linguistics, music, business, politics, and ethics. ENTJs thrive when they are intellectually challenged and when they can contribute to the learning. They need intellectual freedom and do not like to be told what to do or what to think. They lose interest if learning is not challenging or the teacher is not competent.

At Work

ENTJs are organised and task-focused at work. They set high performance standards for themselves and others. For ENTJs success involves looking for improvement. They like to develop systems and continually look for new perspectives, or new ways to improve what they are doing. ENTJs value their position in the organisation and like recognition for their achievements. They are strategic thinkers and planners with a high need for competence.

ENTJs need the freedom to find their own solutions. They like to influence the organisation they work in. At work they are more interested in achieving goals than social interaction. They can be frustrated by lack of closure or people not meeting deadlines, or by other people seeing them as pushy.

Careers

ENTJs like to be in charge. They enjoy a career that allows them to manage other people, or marshal resources. They enjoy work that involves a lot of strategic planning. Some of the careers that attract ENTJs include project management, administration, marketing, computers, consultant, managing people, sales, organisation development and medicine.

Team Role

ENTJs prefer to work in project teams, rather than work alone. In a team they prefer to be leader and set time frames and goals. They need autonomy and space for thinking, and they need complex problems to solve. In a team they need to be clear about objectives and outcomes, and they need to be respected, rather than liked. Difficulties may arise if there are no clear outcomes, or if there is too much external control.

Leadership Style

ENTJs like to be in charge and to know what's going on. They enjoy working with the big picture, marshalling resources and planning future directions. If they don't have the necessary expertise they will find someone who has it and bring them on to the team. ENTJs can see the outcomes clearly and will push the team towards achieving the goals. They demand high standards from their team. ENTJs systematically organise tasks and people, and often take on a mentoring role.

The strengths of ENTJs include their capacity for envisioning the future of the organisation, their ability to initiate and make things happen and their ability to follow a project through to completion. Difficulties may occur if other people find them intimidating or overpowering, particularly if they become so focused on their goals that they are not flexible when it is necessary.

Stress for the ENTJ

Causes of stress

ENTJs need organisation, autonomy, competence and achievement. They will be stressed by personal failure, by not achieving their goals, by a loss of autonomy or by a lack of competence in themselves or the people they work with.

ENTJs prefer Thinking and Intuition, so much of their stress comes from using their less-preferred functions, Sensing and Feeling. They will be stressed by unclear guidelines, lack of efficiency and having to work with a lot of routine or details. Because they organise with logic they often have difficulty when confronted with strong emotions and injustice, and will be stressed by lack of organisation and having no choices. ENTJs may be irritated by leaders who don't know what they want, and by aimlessness or office politics.

Behaviour under stress

Introverted Feeling is usually the least-developed function of the ENTJ and the one most likely to get out of control under stress. When stressed they may experience strong emotions that might be overwhelming, and will fear losing control. On rare occasions they may lose control and become loud, angry and critical. Generally, however, if ENTJs are angry they will withdraw. When they become very stressed they will often organise more to get things done and may take over the group. They may have trouble sleeping, may become ill or impatient, and they may begin to doubt themselves. They may appear more confident in their abilities than they really are.

If people don't deal with stress they may engage in unhealthy psychological games to reduce the effects of stress. ENTJs who are not coping with stress may shut out all emotions, dismissing them as irrelevant. They may also avoid situations where they feel incompetent. The unconscious reasons for this behaviour are to regain the feeling of being in control and being competent, and to appear competent to others. The long-term effect of this behaviour is that fear of failure will prevent them from learning and lead to incompetence.

How to reduce stress

To reduce stress ENTJs need regular interaction, particularly doing Sensing or Feeling activities, like going to dinner. They may find relaxation tapes helpful and may find it helpful to hold or behold something beautiful. Humour may also be useful for ENTJs. If they feel out of control ENTJs may find it necessary to pay attention to the practical details or make a plan to regain control of the situation. If they are hurt by a friend they may find counselling helpful if they are able to talk about it. In the long-term it is important that ENTJs honour their basic need for competence, organisation and achievement.

Leisure and Recreation

ENTJs usually enjoy activities where they can interact with people, particularly people of different cultures. Some may do physical activities like cycling, walking, surfing, or scuba diving. Some ENTJs find gardening and cooking help them to relax. Some will take up take up an activity like cutting gemstones, which is both challenging and beautiful. ENTJs are competitive and like to know they have mastered the skills they are using, and then may lose interest. They often like listening to talk radio or science programmes or watching the National Geographic channel on television.

ENTJs often enjoy reading at home, but may find it tedious at work. They read quickly, skimming through the book for ideas. They enjoy reading that increases their knowledge and gives insight such as science, psychology, anthropology. They often like old books and may read condensed novels about things that interest them.

ENTJ Devlopment

Childhood (6 - 12 years)

ENTJ children are organised, talkative, direct, imaginative and logical. During childhood they develop their Dominant function, extraverted Thinking, so they tend to organise their world logically. For example, one child organised all her toys according to weight and gender. ENTJs ask lots of questions and can logically argue their point of view even at this age. They are usually outspoken, confident and very interested in problem-solving. They have a high need for achievement and usually do well at school as long as they are motivated. They often enjoy solving logic or mathematics problems for fun. They may be frustrated by a lack of order.

ENTJs are often leaders amongst their friends, organising other children to do things. They will often enjoy reading and conversation, and may enjoy singing, dancing, mythology and imagining. Their favourite activity is often organising, anything.

Adolescence (13 - 20 years)

During adolescence ENTJs develop introverted Intuition so they become more reflective at this time. They have a rich imagination and like to plan well into the future and set goals. They are often involved in activities such as organising the school newspaper, debating, or being a representative on the student council. They become more interested in theories, study and books at this age, and are not as interested in team activities. They often pursue creative activity during this period. They are sensitive to injustice and may speak out against discrimination and may have strong feelings of outrage. Some may become exchange students so they can travel and explore the wider world. ENTJs need autonomy and are quite capable of making their own decisions.

Early Adulthood (20 - 35 years)

During this period the Third function, extraverted Sensing, will develop. Now ENTJs turn their attention to the outer world of reality, facts, details and sensory experience. They will be more observant of details and may engage in activities that stimulate the senses, the sights, sounds, tastes and smells. They may engage in physical exercise and outdoor walks enjoying the sensory experience. They may take up new activities like craft, often designing their own ways of doing things. Sometimes these activities will stimulate them to write in a journal or diary. ENTJs will now be more comfortable living in the present and dealing with reality, and many will tend to focus their attention on achieving goals and obtaining recognition for their effort. There will be a great emphasis at this time on achievement at work as they develop their professional skills.

Midlife (35 - 55 years)

During Midlife the Fourth function, introverted Feeling, emerges so ENTJs will spend more time reflecting and will consider the things they value. At this time they become more accepting of people who are different from themselves and more aware of feeling compassion towards others. They may find that they experience emotions that at time overwhelm them and they will feel very much out of control while this happens. This does pass as they become more comfortable with their deeper feelings and values. ENTJs may look for ways to contribute to helping people or perhaps serving the community. They will still base decisions more on logic, but will now begin to take into account the impact their decisions may have on others. It must feel right. They will place more value on time, family and holidays and less on work. At this time issues of relationships and intimacy will become more important for the ENTJ.

ESTJ

Order of Functions:	Dominant	Te
	Auxiliary	Si
	Tertiary	Ne
	Inferior	Fi
Temperament:	Guardian (SJ)	

Strengths

ESTJs are outspoken, practical, systematic and responsible people who like to get the job done right the first time. They are dutiful and persistent guardians. They like to maintain traditions and are very loyal to friends and family.

The Dominant function of ESTJs is extraverted Thinking so they base their decisions on logic. They like order, structure, routine and predictability. ESTJs are very task-focused. They love to organise and tend to rely on other people's ideas and vision. Their supporting function is introverted Sensing, so they are observant and often recall sensory details from past. They trust experience and work well with detail. They are realistic, neat and tidy, and are good at handling logistics.

Potential difficulties

ESTJs find it difficult to function if there is a lack of organisation, if goals are unclear, or if they work too long on their own. Their less-preferred functions are extraverted Intuition and introverted Feeling, so they are not always sensitive to the impact of their decisions on people, and may have difficulty understanding emotions. They may not see the possibilities, and often focus on what might go wrong. They resist change until they see evidence that it will work better in practice.

Communication

The language of ESTJs is detailed, logical and literal. Their Thinking function is extraverted so they tend to explain things logically and provide facts to support their view. They ask a lot of questions to get information, and they like to give a detailed explanation. ESTJs like specific instructions and may have difficulty with symbols and metaphors. In discussions they want closure and solutions, rather than exploration. They usually have a very dry sense of humour which may not be obvious unless you know them well. They sometimes forget to communicate at a personal level, and they rarely talk about feelings. If you want to change their ideas or behaviour then provide evidence and logical reasons for wanting the change. When there is proof they will change quickly.

Relationships

In relationships ESTJs like excitement and predictability, and need honest communication and affection. They like to talk a lot and often ask for logical reasons for what's happening. They control their emotions and don't talk about feelings, even to family and friends. You have to spend a lot of time with them to know how they feel. ESTJs analyse their feelings internally, but often do not tell anyone. People often confide in ESTJs and they don't give away confidences.

Some young ESTJs don't like to be hugged and may have difficulty understanding affection. As they become adult they become more comfortable with affection. ESTJs often take on traditional roles in the family and have a strong sense of responsibility. Some ESTJ women worry unduly about not being good enough as a mother. ESTJs express feeling by what they do. They structure the world to care for you.

Learning

ESTJs learn through experience and are more interested in practical application than theory. They need interaction so they often ask questions to get clarity. Because they perceive mainly through their senses they need the practical experience first, or the theory won't make sense. They have a good memory for things they find interesting. ESTJs use and interpret language literally. They have difficulty if asked to imagine or write about something they have not experienced and may have difficulty interpreting symbolic information. They often dislike writing about abstract issues. They will achieve more if the work is related to real life, if instructions are specific and if they respect the instructor as competent.

ESTJs prefer practical, reality-based subjects like physics, chemistry, mathematics, woodwork, industrial arts, history, home science and sport. They are conscientious students who willingly do homework and practise to improve their skills. They thrive in classes where there is order, routine and feedback, and are easily bored if the work is not relevant to them.

At Work

ESTJs are hard-working and task-focused at work. They do things in a traditional way and they trust what they know from experience. They value organisation and order, and they plan thoroughly. They are reliable and systematic, and work step by step until a task is completed. They make lists of things to achieve and due dates, then revise the lists regularly. They will be frustrated by lack of closure or people not meeting deadlines. ESTJs are motivated by power, prestige and money.

ESTJs prefer to work with other people and focus on one or a few tasks at a time. They are practical and realistic, and can work with a lot of detail. They want lots of interaction but are not usually interested in social interaction at work. Many ESTJs find change difficult unless it happens in small steps. They need evidence to support change and need to believe in it.

Careers

ESTJs at work need challenge, variety and opportunities for leadership. Careers that often interest ESTJs include project management, industrial relations, secretarial, administration, airline pilot, organisation development, quality control, trades, logistics, business management, biochemistry, vocational education, military and electrical or mechanical engineering.

Team Role

ESTJs like cohesive work teams. They are organised and work well with detail and logistics. ESTJs plan and organise tasks easily, and keep to the plan, even under pressure. They are hard-working and reliable. In a team they need to be clear about objectives and accountability, and need to be respected, rather than liked. Difficulties may arise if there is no clear work plan to follow and there are no clear outcomes.

Leadership Style

ESTJ leaders are good at driving initiatives. They often restructure the workplace to make it run more efficiently. They establish expectations, then talk detail. They will focus on getting the job done correctly, and on time. ESTJs create stability, providing clear work plans, roles and procedures, and definite outcomes. They are conscious of time constraints and can systematically organise task and people. They tend to know a lot of information about the organisation.

The strengths of ESTJs include their ability to organise and follow through to completion, their attention to detail, and their concern for justice in the workplace. Difficulties may occur if they take over and don't allow others any autonomy, if they are not sensitive to people's feelings, if they are too sensitive to criticism, or if they resist new ideas.

Stress for the ESTJ

Causes of stress

ESTJs need structure, order, interaction and belonging. They will be stressed by working alone, strong emotions, lack of efficiency or information, and fear of being out of control.

Since ESTJs prefer Thinking and Sensing, much of their stress comes from using the less-preferred functions, Intuition and Feeling .They will be stressed by vague instructions, too many options, unclear guidelines, lack of attention to detail and rapid change. They organise with logic, so they may have difficulty dealing with strong emotions, injustice, insubordination and lack of organisation. They may be irritated by people who don't take them seriously or with people who disregard customs and rules, don't work hard, or don't tell the truth.

Behaviour under stress

Introverted Feeling is usually the least developed function of the ESTJ and the one most likely to get out of control under stress. When they become stressed they will simply work harder, looking at all the information and then formulating a plan to get things done. They put their heads down and work. When they are over-stressed ESTJs may experience very strong emotions that might feel overwhelming, and will fear losing control. On rare occasions they may lose control and become very explosive, angry and critical. Generally however, ESTJs remain in control.

If people don't deal with stress they may engage in unhealthy psychological games to reduce the effects of stress. ESTJs who are not coping with stress will complain, nag, criticise or become depressed. Or, they may feel the stress as physical pain in the body. The unconscious reason for this behaviour is to manipulate others into giving them what they want so that they feel a sense of belonging. The long term effect is that this behaviour often drives people away and they will lose their sense of belonging.

How to reduce stress

To reduce stress ESTJs need regular interaction and time to relax. Some ESTJs can consciously talk themselves into a relaxed state. If they have too much to do, ESTJs will find it helpful to focus on the outcome they want and work steadily, step by step. If the stress is from negative thoughts, they may find it helpful to engage in physical exercise like walking to relax. They sometimes find reading or meditation helpful. In the long-term, it is important that ESTJs let people know about their accomplishments and their needs. To be healthy and manage their stress it is essential that they honour their basic needs for structure and belonging.

Leisure and Recreation

ESTJs will usually enjoy leisure activities that involve some interaction with people, but if they want to relax or exercise they will often do it alone. They are competitive and like to know they have mastered the skills they are using, even in leisure activities. They will often lose interest after they have mastered something. ESTJs enjoy sport such as golf, tennis, swimming, or running. They enjoy holidaying somewhere that is unusual so they can talk about it. They often enjoy tinkering with things, building, remodelling or fixing things. Some other interests may include cooking, crossword puzzles, scrabble, collecting model cars and watching movies about real life.

ESTJs enjoy reading, especially books on practical subjects and biographies such as Angela's Ashes. They often find the imagery in novels like Sons and Lovers difficult. They may also read books on travel, cooking or technical areas related to their hobbies. They will usually organise their books or magazines in alphabetical order or chronological order.

ESTJ Development

Childhood (6 - 12 years)

ESTJ children are organised, outspoken and logical. During childhood they develop their Dominant function, extraverted Thinking, so they are very curious and want logical reasons for what they are told to do. Their decisions are based on logical analysis, not the desire to please anyone. They like to give directions but may be reluctant to follow directions from others. They are often outspoken and will readily express their disagreement with the opinions of adults. ESTJs organise their belongings and keep everything in its right place. They have a high need for achievement and activity, and usually do well at school unless they become bored with it.

ESTJs are realistic and are often leaders amongst their friends. They find it hard to understand why people hug each other and why some children have make-believe play. ESTJs like practical activities like sport, computers, games, making or collecting things, music and helping parents with practical things around the home. Even in play they like to be in charge.

Adolescence (13 - 20 years)

During adolescence ESTJs develop introverted Sensing so they tend to be more reflective and enjoy doing practical things like collecting, sorting, classifying, making or repairing things. They may enjoy sport such as hockey, basketball, athletics, tennis, or other active pursuits like tap dancing, jazz ballet or playing a musical instrument. They are cooperative and very responsible and are often chosen as class captain or class prefect. They take their responsibilities seriously. During this time the ESTJs organise their schoolwork and study time to complete work on time. ESTJs still need interaction so they usually have a good social life. They are often sensitive to injustice and will stand up against bullies. ESTJs need to be responsible and need the opportunity to develop competence.

Early Adulthood (20 - 35 years)

The Third function, extraverted Intuition, develops during this time. Now ESTJs will begin to find change interesting and will often find discussions stimulating. They enjoy hearing ideas and possibilities they could not generate on their own. They may begin to try new things such as different food. They may also begin to miss details and become forgetful and absent-minded as their imagination becomes more active. ESTJs in their twenties are usually very busy and may not spend much time reflecting until they approach midlife. They often join sport or social groups and may become involved as volunteers in community organisations. ESTJs may experience an increase in creativity at this time, with new inspirations and hunches. They may spend time daydreaming about the future.

Midlife (35 - 55 years)

During Midlife the Fourth function, introverted Feeling, emerges. ESTJs will spend more time reflecting on and considering the things they value. At this time they become more accepting of people who are different from themselves and more aware of feeling compassion towards others. They may find that they experience emotions that at times overwhelm them and they may feel out of control while this happens. This does pass as they become more comfortable with their deeper feelings and values. ESTJs will still base decisions more on logic, but they will now begin to take into account the impact their decisions may have on others. It must feel right. They will place more value on time, family and holidays and less on work. At this time issues of relationships and intimacy become more important for the ESTJ. They will often read books on personal development, or even write them.

ISFJ

Order of Functions:	Dominant	Si
	Auxiliary	Fe
	Tertiary	Ti
	Inferior	Ne
Temperament:	Guardian (SJ)	

Strengths

ISFJs are practical, organised and private people who want to take care of others and build a supportive community. They are often seen as caretakers or guardians. They like to maintain traditions and are very loyal to friends and family.

The Dominant gift of ISFJs is introverted Sensing, so they are practical and realistic. They trust what they know from experience and have a great capacity for recalling sensory details from past. For the ISFJ, the past shapes the present. The supporting function of ISFJs is extraverted Feeling so they want to help and support people. They love pleasing people and creating harmony. ISFJs plan everything to ensure that people's needs are met and tasks get done. They tend to be neat and tidy at home and at work.

Potential difficulties

ISFJs find it difficult to function without harmony and support. Their less-preferred functions are introverted Thinking and extraverted Intuition, so they usually find it difficult to deal with conflict and to argue logically. They may withdraw rather than assert themselves. They may try too hard to please others or win their approval. They have difficulty saying 'No' and will usually put other people's needs before their own. ISFJs may have difficulty seeing possibilities and solutions. They often underestimate themselves.

Communication

ISFJs want to connect with people, often preferring to write or telephone. Their language is detailed, friendly and literal. They like to know a lot of details, so they ask a lot of questions. ISFJs like clear and specific instructions and may have difficulty with symbols and metaphors. They are very affirming of others but, being private people, they may not share their own needs and feelings. ISFJs will often initiate interaction so that they can connect with people and like to give advice and opinions about things. They dislike conflict or debate and often agree with people to keep the peace. If you want to change their ideas or behaviour gently suggest the change and show the practical need for it or its affect on people.

Relationships

ISFJs are reserved and don't readily share their emotions, so they take time to get to know. They worry about what people need and show their care by doing things more than by words or hugs. They are supportive and nurturing of others and they thrive on affection and affirmation. In close relationships they need trust and want to be valued as a person. Because they are reliable and do so much for others they are often taken for granted, and then become disappointed. Many ISFJs have close friends that they have known since childhood.

ISFJs put family before themselves and are conscientious about being a good parent or partner. They often take on a traditional role in the family and have a strong sense of responsibility. At home they use candles, colour, lighting and photographs to create a warm atmosphere. The Feeling function of the ISFJs is extraverted so they like to maintain harmony and often avoid confrontation.

Learning

ISFJs learn through experience and learn best in a supportive environment. Because they perceive mainly through their senses, they need practical experience before the theory, or the theory won't make sense. They have a good memory for facts, especially facts about people. Many ISFJs have difficulty if they are asked to imagine and write about something they have not experienced. They will achieve more if the work is related to real life and instructions are specific. They often find visual aids helpful.

ISFJs usually prefer subjects that are practical or based on reality, such as history, geology, biology, woodwork, craft, home economics, music, drama, dance and sport. They are usually very conscientious students who willingly do homework and practise to improve their skills. They are often talkative in a classroom, but prefer to study alone. They fit well into the school system because they are cooperative and love rules, structure, timetables and uniforms. They thrive in classes where there is harmony and good rapport with the teacher.

At Work

ISFJs are hard-working and need structure and harmony in the workplace. They work diligently behind the scenes and will do whatever task they are given. They usually value the traditional ways of doing things and trust what they know from experience. ISFJs plan thoroughly, are reliable and systematic, and work step by step until a task is completed. They can work with a lot of detail and are practical and realistic.

ISFJs care for the people they work with and want to help them. They need affirmation and support and give the same to others. They find performance appraisals difficult and are often stressed by conflict. They respect authority so if they have a problem with their employer they will often leave. Many ISFJs find change difficult unless it happens in small steps.

Careers

ISFJs like a career where they can be of service to people or to the community. They like careers where they can teach or organise or care for people in a practical way. They learn skills quickly and create a warm friendly climate. Common careers for ISFJs include nursing, teaching, family doctor, vocational education, human resources, secretary, administration, small business, trades, coaching, counselling and hospitality.

Team Role

ISFJs take a personal interest in their team members and give constant encouragement. They create harmony, attend to the practical details and ensure that projects are completed on time. They need clear instructions and often need to be invited to share their ideas. Difficulties may arise if they take on too much work, or if there is no clear workplan to follow.

Leadership Style

ISFJs would often prefer to be the second-in-charge rather than the leader. If they do take on a leadership role they will often see it as serving other people. As leaders they focus on helping people achieve and work together cooperatively. They often build a friendly family atmosphere at work. They create stability, providing clear work plans and procedures, and clear and definite outcomes. They can see solutions and what needs to be done, but may have difficulty delegating tasks if they think it will create hardship for someone else.

The strengths of ISFJs include their ability to organise and follow through, their attention to detail, and their support of their staff. Difficulties may occur if they avoid conflict and do not assert themselves when necessary, if they don't allow others enough autonomy, if they forget to delegate, or if they focus too much on the reality and resist new ideas.

Stress for the ISFJ

Causes of stress

ISFJs need structure, order and privacy, and need to belong to a supportive family or group. They will be stressed by too much interacting with people, lack of harmony, conflict, or the fear of negative possibilities.

Since ISFJs prefer Sensing and Feeling, much of their stress comes from using the less-preferred functions, Thinking and Intuition. They will be stressed by vague instructions, too many options, unclear guidelines and indecision. They often have difficulty being assertive or dealing with conflict, and are often sensitive to criticism from others. ISFJs may be irritated by people who disregard customs and rules, are aggressive or patronising, or who take them for granted.

Behaviour under stress

Extraverted Intuition is usually the least developed function of the ISFJ and the one most likely to get out of control under stress. When stressed the ISFJ will often worry constantly about the negative possibilities, what might go wrong, and may have negative thoughts about themselves which can lead to depression. But, if change is required they will force themselves to do it. Under great stress they find it difficult to see the next step. Sometimes they will get angry. Often they will withdraw and may cry on their own. If they are criticised or hurt, ISFJs will often push people away and may experience physical pain from muscle tension. They may feel like nobody cares about them and their world is falling apart.

If people don't deal with stress they may engage in unhealthy psychological games to reduce the effects of stress. ISFJs who are not coping with stress will often complain, nag or become depressed, or they may feel the stress as physical pain in the body. The unconscious reason for this behaviour is to manipulate others into giving them attention so they feel a sense of belonging. The long term effect is that this often drives people away and they lose their sense of belonging.

How to reduce stress

To reduce stress ISFJs need regular time alone to re-focus their attention. If they have too much to do, some ISFJs find it helpful to focus on what they are doing and work steadily, step by step. If the stress is from negative thoughts, they may find it helpful to focus their attention elsewhere, such as the home or the future, or to look at the funny side and laugh. They may find that music, contact with nature or relaxation exercises helpful. It is important that ISFJs learn to be assertive and let people know about their accomplishments. To be healthy and manage their stress it is essential that ISFJs honour their basic needs for structure and belonging.

Leisure and Recreation

ISFJs often enjoy private time, but their extraverted Feeling leads them to want to connect with other people, especially family and friends. They love nature and the outdoors and much of their recreation will involve being in water, in the bush or on a quiet island. ISFJs also enjoy physical activities like swimming, dancing, basketball, golf, walking or soccer. They also enjoy watching sport or coaching others to play sport. ISFJs often enjoy organising a garden, planting in rows, and especially roses. ISFJs also enjoy indoor activities like craft, cooking, playing Bridge, knitting, playing music, collecting things like porcelain dolls, watching ballet and putting photos in an album. Most ISFJs find it difficult to sit and do nothing.

ISFJs often enjoy reading or watching movies about people they can connect with, especially people who overcome obstacles. They often enjoy travel books, biographies and historical novels by authors like Wilbur Smith.

ISFJ Development

Childhood (6 - 12 years)

ISFJ children are quiet, obedient, caring and responsible. During childhood ISFJs develop introverted Sensing so they are usually realistic and enjoy doing practical things. They often find it difficult to imagine and make up stories or games. They would prefer to play games that already have rules. Some ISFJs are very involved in sporting groups or organisations like the Scouts or Guides, and often become leaders. They will often receive awards for achievement or for their responsible behaviour. ISFJ children may seem much more grown up and responsible than other children their age. They enjoy doing things for people or helping around the home.

ISFJ children often enjoy activities like reading, swimming, making things, cooking, knitting, dancing, playing a musical instrument, sports and helping their parents. They sometimes keep their favourite toy well into adulthood. They like books about real life stories or facts, more than fantasy.

Adolescence (13 - 20 years)

Extraverted Feeling develops during adolescence, so ISFJ children are more outgoing and need to care for and interact with people. They enjoy helping people and looking after children and animals. ISFJs like to organise their belongings and keep everything in its right place. Books are often on the shelf in alphabetical order. They work hard at high school and generally do well. They will organise their schoolwork and study time to complete work on time. ISFJs are cooperative and take responsibilities seriously. They could easily be described as the "Best -behaved" child. During adolescence some ISFJs will read biographies or historical novels, rather than fiction. ISFJs generally have a good social life during this time, but many of their activities will focus on family.

Early Adulthood (20 - 35 years)

During this period the Third function, introverted Thinking, emerges. ISFJs will spend a lot of time thinking things through, analysing situations and making more logical decisions as they become more independent. Now they can recognise that some decisions need to be logical and they are not so fearful of the conflict that may result. Now they are more able to give clear instructions with logical reasons and give objective feedback, even to those in authority. Some ISFJs will question rules and the beliefs they have lived by. The caring personality of the ISFJ continues but, as the Thinking emerges, they will consider their own needs before they agree to something. They will become more assertive and less concerned about offending others as they begin to take charge of their own lives and feel a greater sense of freedom to be themselves.

Midlife (35 - 55 years)

During Midlife the Fourth function, extraverted Intuition, develops. Now ISFJs will focus more on the possibilities for the present and the future. They may begin to enjoy discussions and brainstorming more than they did before. They may also begin to miss some details and become forgetful and even absent-minded as the imagination becomes more active. They may begin to put things off until the last minute, but will still meet the deadlines. They may find that they can see meaning in symbols more easily. Some ISFJs may develop an interest in meditation and fantasy. ISFJs may experience a new kind of creativity at this time, innovation. They may experience new inspirations and hunches and spend time daydreaming about the future. This is often a time of change in lifestyle or career as ISFJs become more aware of own their identity, separate from others.

ISTJ

Order of Functions:	Dominant	Si
	Auxiliary	Te
	Tertiary	Fi
	Inferior	Ne

Temperament: Guardian (SJ)

Strengths

ISTJs are private, practical, systematic responsible people who can be relied on to get the job done. They are often seen as protectors or guardians. They like to maintain traditions and are very loyal to friends and family.

The Dominant function of ISTJs is introverted Sensing, so they are quiet observers who can work well with detail. They are practical and realistic. They trust what they know from experience and have a great capacity for recalling sensory details from past. They bring the past into the present. The supporting function of ISTJs is extraverted Thinking so they are decisive and base their decisions on logic. ISTJs are task-focused and hard-working. They like order, structure, routine and predictability. They are neat and tidy at home and at work.

Potential difficulties

ISTJs find it difficult to function if there is a lack of organisation, too much noise and disruption or unclear goals. Their less-preferred functions are introverted Feeling and extraverted Intuition. They are not always sensitive to the impact of their decisions on people, and have difficulty understanding people. They may have difficulty seeing possibilities, and may focus only on what might go wrong. ISTJs will resist change until they see evidence that it will work better.

Communication

The language of ISTJs is usually detailed, logical and literal. Their Thinking function is extraverted so they tend to explain things logically and provide factual information to support their view. They like to give a full and detailed explanation. They like clear and specific instructions and may have difficulty with symbols and metaphors. They will often prefer to listen or to communicate in writing, such as email. In discussions they want closure and solutions, rather than exploration. ISTJs usually have a very dry sense of humour which may not be obvious unless you know them well. They don't often initiate interaction and rarely talk about feelings. If you want to change their ideas or their behaviour provide evidence and logical reasons for wanting the change, then give them time to think about it. When there is evidence, they will change quickly.

Relationships

ISTJs have definite rules regarding relationships. They want consistency, loyalty and truth in their relationships. They need to be able to predict where the relationship is going, based on what is going on in the present. If someone breaks their trust they will sever the relationship permanently, and often will not think about that person again. ISTJs often take on a traditional role in the family and have a strong sense of responsibility.

ISTJs tend to control their emotions, and generally don't talk about their feelings, even to family and friends. They don't cry at funerals, but will cry alone. Often their family and friends don't really know them well. ISTJs express their feelings by what they do. They will work hard to provide security for the family, or will collect money at work to buy a gift for someone who is leaving. ISTJs structure the world to take care of you.

Learning

ISTJs learn through experience and often prefer to work alone. They have a good memory for facts, and details. Because they perceive mainly through their senses they need practical experience before the theory, otherwise the theory won't make sense. ISTJs often have difficulty if they are asked to imagine or write about something they have not experienced. They tend to use and interpret language literally and may have some difficulties with symbols and metaphors. ISTJs will achieve more if the work is related to real life, if the instructions are specific, and if the instructor is competent.

ISTJs usually prefer subjects that are practical or based on reality such as chemistry, mathematics, woodwork, industrial arts and sport. They are conscientious students who willingly do homework and practise to improve their skills. They fit well into the school system because they are cooperative and like rules, structure, timetables and uniforms. They thrive in classes where there is order, routine and feedback.

At Work

ISTJs are hard-working and task-focused at work. They highly value organisation and order, and want clear work roles and procedures. They usually do things in a traditional way and trust what they know from experience. They plan thoroughly. Everything is laid out and organised systematically, and then recorded carefully. They are reliable and systematic, and work step by step until a task is completed. They will be frustrated by lack of closure or people not meeting deadlines.

ISTJs prefer to work alone and focus on one task at a time. They are practical and realistic and can work with a lot of detail. They are not usually interested in social interaction at work. Many ISTJs find change difficult unless it happens in small steps. They need evidence before they agree to change.

Careers

ISTJs often like to work with detailed information, matching performance with some standard, or collecting information, cross checking it and looking for inconsistencies. Common careers for ISTJs include administration, trades, organisation development, military, small business management, auditing, accounting, vocational education, traffic police, secretary, law, forensics and engineering.

Team Role

ISTJs would often prefer to work alone, rather than in a team. In a team they are diligent, hard-working, reliable and very protective. They can plan and organise tasks easily, and will stick to the plan even under pressure. To function in a team they need clear instructions, and need to be respected rather than liked. Difficulties may arise if there is no clear work plan to follow, or if they have several tasks to do at the same time.

Leadership Style

ISTJs would often prefer to be the second-in-charge rather than the leader. If they do take on a leadership role they will focus on making sure the job is done correctly, and on time. They create stability, providing clear work plans, roles and procedures, and definite outcomes. They are natural administrators and enjoy that role. They are very conscious of time constraints and can systematically organise tasks and people. They know a lot of information about the organisation.

The strengths of ISTJs include their ability to organise and follow through to completion, their attention to detail, their ability to concentrate for hours, and their concern for justice in the workplace. Difficulties arise if they do not communicate sufficiently with staff, if they are not sensitive to disharmony, if they don't allow enough autonomy, or if they resist new ideas.

Stress for the ISTJ

Causes of stress

ISTJs need structure, order, privacy, and belonging. They will be stressed by too much interaction and noise, by strong emotions, lack of organisation, and fear of losing control.

Since ISTJs prefer Sensing and Thinking, much of their stress comes from using the less-preferred functions, Feeling and Intuition. They will be stressed by vague instructions, too many options, unclear guidelines, rapid change and by a lack of attention to detail. Because they organise with logic they will often have difficulty dealing with strong emotions, injustice and insubordination. They are usually irritated by people who disregard customs and rules, people who are aggressive or patronising, and people who take them for granted.

Behaviour under stress

Extraverted Intuition is usually the least developed function of the ISTJ and the one most likely to get out of control under stress. When stressed the ISTJ will often worry constantly about the negative possibilities, what might go wrong, and may have negative thoughts about themselves which can lead to depression. Under great stress they find it difficult to see the next step. If change is required they will often force themselves to do it. Sometimes they will get angry. Often they will withdraw and may cry on their own. If they have too many things to do they will work late, or stay up late, until it is all under control. They will be dutiful and persistent.

If people don't deal with stress they may engage in unhealthy psychological games to reduce the effects of stress. ISTJs who are not coping with stress will complain, nag or become depressed. They may feel stress as physical pain in the body, such as headaches. The unconscious reason for this is to manipulate others into giving them attention so they feel a sense of belonging. The long term effect is that this behaviour drives people away and they lose the sense of belonging.

How to reduce stress

To reduce stress ISTJs need regular time alone to re-focus their attention. If they have too much to do, some ISTJs find it helpful to focus on what they are doing and work steadily, step by step. If the stress is from negative thoughts, they may find it helpful to focus on something else, or use physical exercise like walking or controlled breathing to relax. They may find that music, or contact with nature is helpful. In the long-term, it is important that ISTJs let people know about their accomplishments and their needs. To be healthy and manage their stress it is essential that they honour their basic needs for structure and belonging.

Leisure and Recreation

ISTJs will often enjoy spending time alone reading or doing physical activity. They often play competitive sport, and treat it like a job, with things to do while you have fun. They enjoy being in nature, bushwalking or swimming, and like physical activities such as cycling, dancing, basketball, golf, hockey or soccer. They enjoy watching sport or coaching others to play sport. ISTJs often enjoy organising a garden, planting rows of vegetables or flowers. They enjoy indoor activities like craft, cooking, making or repairing things, playing music, sewing and collecting things like stamps or rocks. ISTJs like holidays and travel and usually enjoy the planning. They often return to restaurants and holiday places they have enjoyed.

ISTJs enjoy reading biographies, travel, technical books about their hobbies, books on social phenomena or ethics, and books about people who set goals and achieve them, such as Scott's expedition to the Antarctic. ISTJs enjoy classic movies such as *Casablanca* and comedy like the *Three Stooges* or *Seinfeld*.

ISTJ Development

Childhood (6 - 12 years)

ISTJ children are quiet, obedient, observant and responsible. During childhood ISTJs develop introverted Sensing so they are practical and enjoy doing things or making things. They like order and predictability and will put things away and even straighten the rugs on the floor. They often seem much more grown up and responsible than other children their age. Some ISTJs are involved in sporting groups or organisations like Scouts or Guides, and often receive awards for achievement or responsible behaviour. ISTJ children are realistic and practical and find it difficult to imagine and make up stories or games. They would prefer games that have definite rules.

ISTJ children usually enjoy activities like reading, swimming, making things, cooking, knitting, dancing, playing a musical instrument, sports and helping their parents at home. Many ISTJs collect things like stamps, football cards or rocks. They like books about real life stories or facts, more than fantasy.

Adolescence (13 - 20 years)

During this period the extraverted Thinking emerges. ISTJs spend a lot of time organising, planning and making logical decisions. They like to organise their belongings and keep everything in its right place. Books are often on the shelf in alphabetical order. They work hard at high school and they generally do well. They will organise their schoolwork and study time to complete work on time. ISTJs are cooperative and take their responsibilities seriously. During this time ISTJs will often read technical or scientific books, more than fiction. Much of their social life will focus on family. ISTJs at this age are outspoken and assertive and can readily explain decisions and argue their viewpoint logically. They usually have a strong sense of justice and fairness. They often hold positions of responsibility at school like class captain.

Early Adulthood (20 - 35 years)

Introverted Feeling develops during this period so ISTJs will spend more time reflecting and considering the things they value. They may find that they experience emotions that at times overwhelm them, and they will feel very much out of control while this happens. At this time they become more accepting of people who are different from themselves and more aware of feeling compassion towards others. They will often volunteer their time to work in a community service organisation, usually one that follows traditional values. The ISTJ at this time will still base decisions more on logic, but will now begin to take into account the impact their decisions may have on others. At this time issues around relationships and intimacy become very important for the ISTJ.

Midlife (35 - 55 years)

At Midlife the Fourth function, extraverted Intuition, develops. ISTJs will tend to focus more on possibilities and will be less concerned about rules or customs. They usually want more autonomy, want more out of life and want more personal development. For many, this is a time of soul-searching as they become more aware of themselves and their potential. Some ISTJs will enjoy discussions and brainstorming more than before. They may also begin to miss details and become forgetful and absent-minded as the imagination becomes more active. They may see meaning in symbols more easily. At this time they often become more flexible and less concerned with deadlines and timetables, though they will still meet the deadlines. This is often a time of change in lifestyle or career as the ISTJs become more aware of their own identity and more concerned about the balance between work and family life.

- 31

INFJ

Order of Functions	Dominant	Ni
	Auxiliary	Fe
	Tertiary	Ti
	Inferior	Se
Temperament:		Idealist (NF)

Strengths

INFJs are reflective, imaginative, caring and idealistic. Their life is a quest for meaning and authenticity. They have strong intuitions about inner reality and focus their energy on helping people to reach their potential. They are private and independent.

The Dominant gift of INFJs is introverted Intuition, so they generate new ideas quickly, preferably on their own. They see into the present, the central images in a story, its consequences and possible outcomes. This intuition works in the areas where they have immersed themselves. They value the imaginative activity of people, the symbols, images, stories, myths and dreams. Their supporting function is extraverted Feeling so they value people and the interconnectedness of life in all its forms, and are committed to helping people to reach their potential.

Potential difficulties

INFJs are at home in their inner world and often feel their energy is drained away by extraverted behaviour. The less-preferred functions of the INFJ are introverted Thinking and extraverted Sensing, so they may not notice the reality or details around them. They sometimes seize one idea and make a decision too quickly. They may try too hard to please others or win their approval and may avoid dealing with conflict.

Communication

INFJ language tends to be focused on concepts and feelings. They sometimes find speaking difficult because the ideas come so fast and may be impossible to keep up with. In discussions they are often the last to speak because they need to remain open to get as complete a picture as possible. Sometimes they don't hear what other people are saying because they are lost in their inner world. INFJs are open to people, but few people will know their centre. They usually prefer to write, crafting words to touch people's hearts.

INFJs are private people, preferring in-depth conversations with a person they know, or writing in diaries, in journals or poetry. They dislike too many details, and want only enough to reveal the overall pattern. If you want to change their ideas or behaviour tell them how their actions are affecting or hurting you. If they trust you they will do all they can to change.

Relationships

INFJs need authentic relationships, to be able to share some of the inner self and have it reciprocated. They enjoy one-to one relationships but will only let those they trust into their inner world. Family is very important to INFJs, the source of strength. They need a spiritual connection to their partner, to be a soul friend. They enjoy nurturing and playing with children.

People often confide in INFJs. INFJs know the importance of listening to a person's story. They are sensitive to other people's suffering and can become very emotional while listening to someone's personal story. The Feeling function of INFJs is extraverted so they like to maintain harmony. They may avoid confrontation by withdrawing, but will confront an issue if their values are violated.

Learning

INFJs are imaginative, conceptual and independent learners. As their introverted Intuition develops during childhood they tend to be imaginative and like theories and concepts. They work best when inspired and enjoy learning that stimulates the imagination or reveals patterns or the dynamics behind events. They can memorise huge amounts of information by seeing the overall pattern and making picture summaries and flow diagrams. They are keen readers, have very good language skills and usually excel in subjects where they are able to express their ideas in written form.

INFJs usually do well academically. They are often attracted to learning in areas such as history, archaeology, art, mythology, music, mathematics, science, languages, psychology, poetry and other forms of writing. They set very high standards for their work, tend to be perfectionists. INFJs will lose interest if the learning does not stimulate the imagination or if there is disharmony.

At Work

At work INFJs want to help people achieve, and will choose the organisation to work for because of its values. They need to work with people. When working on a project INFJs are constantly thinking about how it will benefit someone and how to present it in a way that will connect with people's experiences. They like finding solutions to people-related problems, and believe that looking after the people will ultimately benefit the organisation. They will clash with authority if the work practices are harmful to people or the environment.

INFJs need goals and priorities at work. They are organised and conscientious workers who meet deadlines easily, often in advance. They are not interested in the detail unless it is important for seeing the patterns. If the job becomes repetitive they will move on. INFJs need harmony and may have difficulty if they try too hard to please others and don't deal with conflict.

Careers

INFJs enjoy work that focuses on growth, well-being and healing. They often take on the role of teacher or therapist and are thrilled when the person they are working with achieves success. INFJs are more concerned with formation than information. They focus on fostering a love of learning in their subject area and in so doing foster a love of all learning. Common careers for INFJs are writing, counselling, church ministry, psychology, education, training, child development, art, social work and health.

Team Role

INFJs are caring team members who inspire and harmonize the group. They often prefer to work alone or in small groups. They understand people and can offer helpful insights. They need harmony, autonomy and some time alone. Difficulties may arise if they work too hard, if they resist the rules of the organisation or if too much interaction drains their energy.

Leadership Style

INFJs are visionary leaders who can inspire their team. Their focus is on accomplishing the task by getting the right people involved. They are not authoritarian, preferring to allow team members some autonomy. They will often take on a mentoring role and can motivate people to want to achieve and work together. They foster harmony in the team and will provide the support for individuals to develop.

The strengths of INFJs include their focus on the development of individual potential, their personal integrity and their ability to vision the present situation and future possibilities. Difficulties may occur if their values conflict with others, if they neglect the practical needs of the organisation, if they are not assertive when necessary, or if they become frustrated by the imperfections in others or the organisation.

Stress for the INFJ

Causes of stress

INFJs need to have meaningful harmonious relationships and know that they are contributing to people's lives. They also need privacy, and may find their energy drained by listening to other people's stories and sharing their suffering. They will also be stressed by conflict, noise, lack of structure or a conflict of values.

Since INFJs prefer Intuition and Feeling, much of their stress comes from using the less-preferred functions, Thinking and Sensing. They are often stressed by routine, details, by being late, and practical things like filing or filling in forms. Too much mess or clutter is also stressful. INFJs often work very hard and may not notice the physical effects on the body. They have difficulty being assertive and are irritated by people who judgemental, manipulative, thoughtless or legalistic.

Behaviour under stress

Extraverted Sensing is usually the least developed function of the INFJ and the one most likely to get out of control under stress. When stressed the INFJ may lose sense of space and details and become confused or focus on unimportant details Often they will withdraw until they work out how to respond. They may go to sleep, watch a lot of TV or cry alone. Under extreme stress INFJs may have angry outbursts, make endless lists or do a lot of physical activity like house cleaning. If this happens they will lose energy and may have problems with insomnia or weight change. They may become emotionally exhausted or even ill, needing long periods of rest.

If people do not deal with stress they may engage in unhealthy psychological games to reduce the effects of stress. INFJs who are not coping with stress may ignore the symptoms or repress their feelings or delude themselves into thinking they are coping. The unconscious reason for this behaviour is to hide their feelings from others and from themselves. The long term effect of this behaviour is that it makes it difficult for them to enter into a meaningful and honest relationship.

How to reduce stress

To reduce stress INFJs will often engage in some physical activity such as walking, yoga or gardening. They need time alone to reflect and may benefit from listening to music, being near the water or nature, and sharing their story with somone. To be healthy and manage their stress, it is essential that INFJs honour their basic needs to find meaning and a sense of their own identity. They often find it helpful to focus on where they are making a difference in the world and the symbols of transformation that help to make sense of where they are in the world.

Leisure and Recreation

INFJs enjoy a variety of leisure activities, preferring activities they can do alone or with a few people. They enjoy activities that stimulate the imagination such as music, writing poetry, photography, art, journaling, reading, daydreaming, meditation, dancing and acting. They enjoy healing, personal growth workshops, retreats, yoga, massage, watching movies or listening to the surf. They may also enjoy walking, surfing, skiing and are often drawn to places of beauty. They may enjoy team or group activities if the group has a strong bond. They often find TV and movies intrusive, preferring to allow images from their own unconscious to emerge. They enjoy films with a lot of symbolism, such as *The Fisher King*, and the humour of *Fawlty Towers*.

INFJs read stories with symbolism or messages about the search for love and meaning. They enjoy myths, legends, poetry and classic novels. They often enjoy having their ideas represented in an irreverent way, such as *Poo and Ancient Greece*. INFJs read detailed crime novels, fascinated by the presence of beauty in the midst of the ugliness of reality.

INFJ Development

Childhood (6 - 12 years)

INFJ children are quiet, independent, sensitive and very imaginative. The Dominant function, introverted Intuition, develops during childhood so they spend a lot of time alone, allowing the imagination to take them to magical kingdoms, far away places, and other worlds. They often have a favourite place in their room or a cubby house where they can be alone. Many INFJ children have imaginary playmates and talk to fairies in the garden. They enjoy making things that are related to their fantasies, drawing images from the imagination or thinking up names for their imaginary friends. They often have intense feelings, like dragons and monsters, that come from the depth that they have to learn to control.

INFJ children enjoy reading books, reading and writing poetry, drama, and dreaming about the future and how things could be better for people. They are not always interested in toys and may remember little of the details of their childhood. They may not be interested in practical tasks and routine.

Adolescence (13 - 20 years)

During adolescence INFJs become more outgoing as they develop their extraverted Feeling. They will often become popular and enjoy parties but will find that the interaction drains their energy. They need to connect with other people at this age and feel very responsible for people. They may become quite distressed when they hear stories of tragedy and suffering. Some will volunteer for community service. At this time their values are developing and they are learning to base decisions on their own personal values. They may begin to question the values of their parents or teachers. INFJs often see their future career as a vocation, focusing on what they can do for others through counselling, teaching or spiritual work. They need autonomy and respond positively to guidance from adults who understand them and encourage them to be themselves. They are often involved in drama, and usually have a good social life, and do well academically.

Early Adulthood (20 - 35 years)

During this period the Third function, introverted Thinking, emerges. INFJs will spend a lot of time thinking things through, analysing situations and making more logical decisions as they become more independent. Now they can logically justify decisions that previously may have been based on 'gut feelings'. They may feel tension between maintaining harmony and following their own beliefs and ideals. The sensitive and caring personality of the INFJ will continue during adulthood, but now the INFJ will often become more assertive, and less concerned about offending others. At times they may even appear aggressive as they begin to take charge of their own lives and feel a greater sense of freedom to be themselves.

Midlife (35 - 55 years)

During Midlife the Fourth function, extraverted Sensing, will develop. Now INFJs turn their attention to the outer reality, of facts, details and sensory experience. They will be more observant of details in nature and may engage in activities that stimulate the senses such as planting trees or lavender, gem collecting, fossicking, sport or carpentry. In some cases these activities will inspire them to write poetry. Sometimes the Sensing is expressed in surprising ways like dancing on the table or mischievous humour. INFJs need to be careful that all this activity does not lead to burnout. INFJs at midlife will be more comfortable living in the present and creating a harmonious environment, removing clutter from their surroundings and using colours that harmonise.

INTJ

Order of Functions:	Dominant	Ni
	Auxiliary	Te
	Tertiary	Fi
	Inferior	Se
Temperament:	Rational (NT)	

Strengths

INTJs are independent, imaginative, logical and private. They have clear visions about inner reality and focus their energy on working to achieve their goals. They thrive on solving complex problems and finding ways to improve things.

The Dominant gift of the INTJ is introverted Intuition, so they see visions of present reality and what's possible in the future. They generate new ideas quickly, preferably on their own. The imagination of INTJs speaks in symbols, images, stories and dreams. Their supporting function is extraverted Thinking so they base their decisions on logic. They enjoy organising and strategic planning to achieve the outcomes they can see. They value justice and competence.

Potential difficulties

INTJs need a lot of time alone and are hard to get to know. They are at home in the inner world and often feel that their energy is drained away by extraverted behaviour. Their less-preferred functions are introverted Feeling and extraverted Sensing, so they may sometimes have difficulty focusing on reality, details and practical tasks. They may have difficulty understanding people and are not always sensitive to the impact of their decisions on people.

Communication

The language of INTJs focuses on concepts and logic. They want conversations to be conceptually stimulating. They sometimes find speaking difficult because the ideas come so fast. They often put their ideas forward strongly so that they are heard and to encourage people to consider and debate other views. INTJs have clear visions of what's possible but may have difficulty expressing what they know. Sometimes they don't hear what other people say because they are lost in their inner world. INTJs are private people, and prefer conversations with someone they know, or writing in diaries or journals. They don't usually like small talk and prefer talking to people they see as competent. If you want to change their ideas or behaviour give logical reasons and focus on the big picture. Be direct and stay focused on the main issues.

Relationships

INTJs respect competence and directness. In a relationship they want the other person to have opinions and ideas. INTJs enjoy one-to-one relationships but take time to get to know. They are sometimes afraid of intimacy, except with family. They are loyal to their friends and often make friends with people who share their interests and often feel more at home with other Thinking types. INTJs usually know at the beginning of a relationship if they will get on with someone.

INTJs feel things deeply but do not usually discuss emotions because they can be overwhelming. At work their feelings may not be obvious because INTJs focus on using their extraverted Thinking to communicate. At home they are more comfortable with feelings and values. They encourage independence in their children and are consistent in how they handle them. They often show they care by problem-solving.

Learning

INTJs are imaginative, conceptual independent learners. They learn best in a challenging environment with regular opportunities for quiet. Their Intuition is introverted so they enjoy abstract concepts and theories. They are strategic thinkers. INTJs value learning for its own sake and enjoy solving complex problems. They focus on the big picture and are not usually interested in the details or in practical applications unless they are needed to help understand the concepts. INTJs are keen readers and usually have very good language skills. They often enjoy the nuance of language, and may also enjoy the structure and sounds of a language like Latin.

INTJs are high achievers who strive for excellence and they usually do well academically. They often enjoy learning in areas such as history, languages, psychology, music, writing, philosophy, religion, information technology, bio-ethics and art. They need intellectual freedom, to think their own thoughts. They lose interest if the learning is not challenging or the teacher is not competent.

At Work

INTJs are strategic thinkers and planners with a high need for competence. They constantly question the structures and rules. They like to develop systems and they are continually looking for ways to improve the way things are done. They set high performance standards for themselves and others. INTJs are confident about their decisions which are logically calculated. They value justice in the workplace. They see each person's job as equally important and give the person respect for competence rather than position.

INTJs need autonomy, the freedom to find their own solutions. They often feel like they carry the weight of the company on their shoulders and are irritated by people who don't appear to work hard. They are organised and task-focused and are frustrated by lack of closure or people not meeting deadlines.

Careers

INTJs are quiet achievers and enjoy careers that involve strategic planning but prefer to focus on visioning more than goals. Some careers that attract INTJs include industrial relations, project management, management, organisational development, information technology, corporate vision consultant, coaching, university teaching and psychology. They like to have the opportunity to create improvement on a big scale.

Team Role

INTJs prefer to work alone or work independently. They often initiate projects and develop strategies. They need a lot of autonomy and quiet for thinking and problem solving. In a team they need clear objectives and outcomes. They need to be respected, more than liked. Difficulties may arise if they have to deal with a lot of detail or if there are no clear goals.

Leadership Style

INTJs don't usually seek to be the leader but others often see them that way. Some like front line leadership or coaching. They enjoy working with the big picture and planning future directions. They can create systems to achieve their goals. They will work out the structure then delegate the tasks, and give a lot of autonomy. INTJs will tend to delegate to the person who has the expertise, regardlesss of age or position.

The strengths of INTJs include their capacity for visioning what is possible, their ability to develop logical systems, and their ability to set goals and follow a project through to completion. Difficulties may occur if other people find them intimidating or overpowering, or if they become so focused on the goals that they are not flexible when necessary.

Stress for the INTJ

Causes of stress

INTJs need privacy, organisation, autonomy and competence. They will be stressed by too much interaction with others, a lack of structure, or by lack of competence in themselves or the other people in the work place.

Since INTJs prefer Intuition and Thinking, much of their stress comes from using their less-preferred functions, Feeling and Sensing. They will be stressed by unclear guidelines, lack of efficiency and having to work with a lot of routine or details. Because they organise with logic they often have difficulty dealing with strong emotions and injustice, and will be stressed by lack of organisation and having no choices. INTJs may be irritated by aimlessness or office politics, or by leaders who don't know what they want.

Behaviour under stress

Extraverted Sensing is usually the least developed function of INTJs and the one most likely to get out of control under stress. When stressed they may lose sense of space and become confused or focus on unimportant details. Often they will withdraw until they work out how to respond. They may be overwhelmed by emotion or haunted by images they can't control. They may become angry and critical, may overeat or obsess about germs. When INTJs are stressed they often don't notice the effects on their bodies. They may become emotionally exhausted or ill, needing long periods of rest.

If people don't deal with stress they may engage in unhealthy psychological games to reduce the effects of stress. INTJs who are not coping with stress may shut out all emotions, dismissing them as irrelevant. They may also avoid situation where they feel incompetent. The unconscious reasons for this behaviour are to regain the feeling of being in control and being competent, and to appear competent to others. The long-term effect of this behaviour is that a fear of failure may prevent them from learning and lead to incompetence.

How to reduce stress

To reduce stress INTJs need regular time alone to reflect and re-focus on the big picture. They will benefit from activities that engage their intuition, like journal writing, meditation, music or looking at something beautiful. If they feel out of control INTJs may find it necessary to pay attention to their emotions and express their feelings and concerns out loud. In the long-term it is important that INTJs honour their basic needs for competence, organisation and achievement.

Leisure and Recreation

INTJs usually enjoy activities they can do on their own or with a few people rather than large groups. Some enjoy outdoor physical activities like walking, carpentry, golf, skiing or sailing. They often enjoy activities that are challenging and require the mastery of some skill, like solo yachting. When they want to unwind they may take on a big project like building a glider. They often find nature relaxing and rejuvenating and, as they enter their mature years, focus more on the details in nature than the thought processes in their mind. INTJs are not high risk takers in leisure and don't usually enjoy parties.

INTJs enjoy reading and writing. They usually prefer reading that increases their knowledge and challenges the mind, such as psychology, science, anthropology, philosophy, murder mysteries or books about the future. Some INTJs prefer Medieval Murder Mysteries because they are set in another time and place, and so are more complex. Some INTJs like old and rare books and some read condensed novels about specific things, such as naval battles. They often like to organise their books in alphabetical order or by author.

INTJ Development

Childhood (6 - 12 years)

INTJ children are quiet, organised, independent and very imaginative. Their Dominant function, introverted Intuition, develops during childhood so they spend a lot of time alone visiting imaginary worlds, such as the land of the Vikings. They may spend many hours alone in their room or on a rocking horse as they visit these far away places and imagine themselves as powerful warriors. People often refer to them as dreamers. They rarely tell anyone about their imaginary life. Some INTJ children see images in familiar things, like faces in the curtains or dogs in the window. They often have intense feelings that come from the depths, such as dragons and monsters, that they have to learn to control.

INTJ children usually enjoy creative activities like reading books, writing poetry, music and drama. They are not usually very interested in toys, practical tasks or routine. They usually remember little of the details of their childhood.

Adolescence (13 - 20 years)

During adolescence INTJs become more outgoing as they develop their extraverted Thinking. They organise their world logically and confidently debate issues with adults, certain that they are right. INTJs at this time are often surprised by their own intellectual ability, as they learn to base their decisions on logic. They will often become leaders in their peer group, and may be elected school or class captain. They are usually concerned with justice issues and at this time may become involved in organising campaigns such as Freedom from Hunger. As they look to a future career they will often see themselves as the boss. They usually do well academically and socially but do not usually enjoy parties. INTJs need autonomy and respond positively to guidance from adults who allow them to be independent.

Early Adulthood (20 - 35 years)

During this period introverted Feeling emerges so INTJs will spend more time reflecting on what they value. At this time they become more accepting of people who are different from themselves and more aware of feeling compassion towards others. They may find that they experience emotions that at times overwhelm them. They will feel very much out of control while this happens. This does pass as they become more comfortable with their deeper feelings and values. INTJs at this time may look for ways to contribute to helping people or perhaps serving the community in some way. They will still base decisions more on logic, but will now begin to take into account the impact their decisions may have on others. It must feel right. They will now place more value on time, family and holidays and less on work. At this time issues of relationships and intimacy will become more important for the INTJ.

Midlife (35 - 55 years)

During Midlife the Fourth function, extraverted Sensing, will develop. Now INTJs turn their attention to the outer world of reality, facts, details and sensory experience. They will be more observant of details and will often engage in activities that stimulate the senses, the sights, sounds and smells. Some may engage in physical exercise and outdoor walks, enjoying the sensory experience. They may become more interested in health and keeping the body in shape. They may take up new activities like craft, often designing their own ways of doing things. Sometimes these activities will stimulate them to write in a journal or diary. INTJs will now be more comfortable living in the present and dealing with reality, but they will still focus on setting and achieving goals and obtaining recognition for their effort. They will still like to live in an orderly way.

ISTP

Order of Functions:	Dominant	Ti
	Auxiliary	Se
	Tertiary	Ni
	Inferior	Fe
Temperament:	Artisan (SP)	

Strengths

ISTPs are reserved, realistic, straightforward and logical. They are good at troubleshooting and negotiating and they like to analyse how things work. ISTPs like to spend a lot of time alone and do not like being the centre of attention. They are adaptable and spontaneous. They seek constant action and need flexibility and freedom in life and work.

The Dominant gift of the ISTP is the introverted Thinking, so they base important decisions on internal logic. They enjoy solving problems, particularly practical, mechanical or technical problems. They often build models or blueprints inside their heads. The supporting function of the ISTP is extraverted Sensing, so they live in the moment and are able to absorb a lot of detailed information from the world around them.

Potential difficulties

The less-preferred functions of the ISTP are introverted Intuition and extraverted Feeling. They may have difficulty seeing the big picture, visioning what is possible or dealing with theory. ISTPs often have difficulty relating to people and expressing how they feel or what they want. They prefer to do rather than talk and may act before thinking an idea through. They often put off tasks that they don't like. If they are bored they will quickly lose interest and may not complete the task.

Communication

ISTPs see much but share little. Their extraverted Sensing focuses on facts and reality in the present situation. They are observant, noticing and remembering details, including body language, but may be irritated by a lot of detail from others. They dislike long explanations, preferring to get to the point quickly. Their language is factual, logical and literal. ISTPs feel vulnerable talking in front of a group, preferring one-to-one conversation. They are often seen as cool and aloof, but see themselves as reserved and discerning about who they will share information with. They talk about their experiences more than how they feel as they are often not comfortable talking about emotions. If you want to change their behaviour you need to give them logical reasons and specific examples, and then negotiate with them unemotionally.

Relationships

In a relationship ISTPs want freedom, independence and a person they can trust. They want a warm, friendly relationship where they are appreciated as they are. They like someone who listens without criticising and dislike emotional outbursts. They will usually avoid confrontation by withdrawing. ISTPs will often ignore social role expectations.

ISTPs usually have a small circle of close friends and often like to be alone. They often have difficulty forming intimate relationships and may feel lonely. People may find it hard to get close to them or may think they don't have feelings. They will share feelings with someone they know and trust. Their Feeling function develops at midlife so ISTPs may find it difficult to express how they feel or even to know what they are feeling before this time.

Learning

ISTPs learn more by doing than by listening and reading. They perceive lots of detailed information through their extraverted Sensing, what they see, touch, taste, hear or smell. ISTPs are curious to know how things work and like to solve problems. Their introverted Thinking develops when they are children and enables them to logically evaluate information. They want to learn quickly and in a classroom will become bored and lose interest if they don't have something to do. ISTPs need a competent teacher and prefer to work on their own.

ISTPs enjoy learning that is practical, useful and hands-on. They like subjects with a very clear rule structure, such as French and chemistry, analytical subjects such as mathematics, science, geometry and sports or sports science. They will read only if the subject interests them, usually adventure stories with lots of movement or books on how things work. ISTP children often find school difficult because they get bored with theory and too much talk from the teacher. They may have difficulty writing essays or if asked to explore the meaning of something or to imagine something they have not experienced. Unless given permission, they may see copying from a book or using the imagination as cheating. They prefer reality.

At Work

ISTPs are lateral thinkers and prefer to have lots of things to do and problems to solve. At work they enjoy a crisis, but get bored with routine and want to move on once a problem is solved. Their quick action may be mistaken for a need for closure, but they don't always finish tasks they start. They like variety and need deadlines to get things finished. ISTPs can work in a structure if there is flexibility within it.

ISTPs focus on getting the job done correctly. They are not impressed by rules, hierarchy, position or status and they will ignore rules if they can't see the logic in them. They like to know that they have the freedom to break the rules if they want to. If they can't see the point in doing something they are unlikely to finish it. They don't like being controlled and like individual responsibility. ISTPs are good at logistics and working with lots of detail. They often prefer to work alone.

Careers

ISTPs are often found in jobs or careers that are active and practical or involve troubleshooting. This may include such areas as technicians and maintenance work, the military, trades, adventure training, private coaching, bio-mechanics, crisis centres, farming, business and professional sport.

Team Role

ISTPs are not natural team members, preferring to work alone. They are suited to total quality management where they have individual responsibility. They are good at analysing problems to find solutions. They are good at asking the right questions so, if they do work in a team, they add clarity of ideas. They like clear targets and the freedom to reach them in their own way.

Leadership Style

ISTPs do not often seek leadership roles. They usually dislike directing others and will not force people to do things. In a crisis they assume leadership and make quick decisions. They lead by example and expect others to follow. ISTPs are more comfortable as leaders than managers.

The strengths of the ISTP are that they can gather and store a lot of information, they can analyse logically, they are pragmatic and get the job done, and they allow people freedom to work without interference. Difficulties may occur if they don't see the big picture, if they don't meet deadlines or if they remain aloof and don't relate well to the people involved.

Stress for the ISTP

Causes of stress
The main causes of stress for the ISTP are related to meeting deadlines, relating with people, especially in groups, and lack of flexibility or freedom. They find it difficult being too long with groups of people, preferring to interact one-to-one. Deadlines are often useful for ISTPs, but will create stress if there is not enough time to do the job well, or if things go wrong and prevent them meeting the deadline. ISTPs may be stressed by having to redo a task after new information is presented.

Much of the stress for ISTPs comes from using their less-preferred functions, Intuition and Feeling. ISTPs may be stressed by people who are narrow-minded, critical, stubborn, emotional or not logical. ISTP's need freedom and they may become stressed by situations or people who are inflexible or controlling. They can also be stressed by too many options or trying to generate possibilities.

Behaviour under stress
ISTPs may become disruptive when stressed or they may withdraw to think things through. When very stressed ISTPs may become emotional and raise their voice or cry, and generally behave in ways that are not rational. They will often become focused on the task, ignoring the people, or may become totally immersed in the problem that is causing the stress. They often engage in manual work to relieve stress.

If people don't deal with serious stress they may engage in unhealthy psychological games to reduce the effects of stress. ISTPs who are not coping with stress may resort to blackmail games such as tantrums or violent outbursts, risky behaviour that may be life-threatening, delinquency, boredom or serious depression. The unconscious reasons for this behaviour are to experience excitement, to feel a sense of freedom, or to punish the person who has taken away their freedom. The long term effect of this behaviour is that ISTPs may lose their freedom as a result of their behaviour.

How to reduce stress
ISTPs often use physical activity such as running or manual work to reduce stress. They will usually withdraw from the company of other people preferring to be alone, and sometimes will relax and do nothing. They are usually able to put off the task until tomorrow. When stressed they need to check the facts and be realistic about the situation, then use their logic to decide what is the appropriate action before they act. To be healthy and manage their stress it is essential that the ISTPs honour their basic need for freedom and action.

Leisure and Recreation
ISTPs often enjoy spending quiet time alone reading, playing sport or doing physical activities where they build, fix, landscape, make or renovate. ISTPs enjoy many sports, such as rowing, soccer, basketball, scuba-diving, white water rafting, fun-runs, parasailing or exercising in a gym. They usually enjoy training and often compete at national or international levels. Their hobbies are varied and include such things as using tools, live theatre, martial arts, fine food and wine, chess, cooking, leadlighting, card games, weaving, gardening, sewing, woodwork, and all kinds of music. ISTPs often enjoy watching sport or documentaries and listening to talkback radio.

ISTPs often enjoy reading books that stimulate their thinking or provide practical information. This may include such topics as science, science fiction, gardening, house renovating, how things work, or books about other cultures. Stories need to be action or adventure stories. ISTPs like to do things well. They will say things like "Do it well or not at all." or "Just do it! "

ISTP Development

Childhood (6 - 12 years)
ISTP children are usually very quiet, active, logical and happy to be alone much of the time. They need activity and a variety of things to do. They trust what is real and interpret language and instructions literally. Their Dominant function, introverted Thinking, develops during this period, so ISTP children will spend time reflecting and analysing internally as they develop their logic. They are particularly interested in understanding how things work, such as how do they get music onto a record? Other people may not see their logical and analytical ability because it happens internally. What others will see is a quiet child who is straightforward, wants to try everything and is happy to spend time alone. ISTPs need flexibility and freedom and lose interest if they don't have something to do.

Favourite activities for ISTP children often include playing sport or watching sport; outdoor activities; making or assembling mechanical things; playing computer games; craft; watching people; using tools; solving mathematical problems. ISTPs are usually competitive at sport and usually prefer individual performance sports. They prefer activity that has a purpose, such as making, solving or fixing things.

Adolescence (13 - 20 years)
During adolescence ISTPs develop extraverted Sensing and are constantly active, taking in vast amounts of information through their senses. They gather facts and details about things. They will put a lot of energy into an activity until they lose interest. Their behaviour during this period may appear extraverted as their activity is focused more in the outer world, but they will still need time alone. ISTPs need freedom and action and will resist control. They will respond positively to guidance from adults they respect. They may find school frustrating because of the emphasis on theory rather than practical work and because much of what they learn is not relevant to them. If conflict arises they will often withdraw or keep their opinions to themselves to avoid any unpleasant confrontation. They rarely, if ever, talk about feelings.

Early Adulthood (20 - 35 years)
During this period the Third function, introverted Intuition, develops. The quiet, logical personality of the ISTP continues throughout adulthood, but now their inner reflections are times of inspiration. They will focus more on possibilities for the future and big picture concepts and theories. They will begin to appreciate symbols and the meaning behind reality. They may pay less attention to the details and practical realities and may find themselves daydreaming and forgetting things. Some ISTPs may be drawn to dream work or meditation as they explore their inner Intuition. They will usually have their best inspirations when they are alone. ISTPs may experience an increase in creativity at this time, becoming more innovative and turning their attention more towards the future.

Midlife (35 - 55 years)
At midlife the ISTP develops extraverted Feeling. During this time they become more sensitive to the feelings of others. They will be more aware of the need to affirm others and will often become more tactful, sometimes sentimental, and more easily hurt. Though they are more interested in personal relationships and intimacy at this time they may still find it hard to get close to others, and may still find emotions a challenge. As the Feeling function develops they will become more aware of how they feel and what is important to them, and the need for harmony. Decisions will now be influenced by their personal values, as well as logic.

INTP

Order of Functions:	Dominant	Ti
	Auxiliary	Ne
	Tertiary	Si
	Inferior	Fe
Temperament:	Rational (NT)	

Strengths

INTPs are reserved, analytical, conceptual, lateral thinkers. They like to spend a lot of time alone and do not like being the centre of attention. They value truth knowledge, and need autonomy and intellectual freedom.

The Dominant gift of the INTP is introverted Thinking, so they base important decisions on internal logic. They like complex, seemingly unsolvable problems and will look at any problem from many different angles before they draw conclusions. INTPs build models or blueprints in their heads, always seeking logical consistency. The supporting function of the INTP is extraverted Intuition so they generate many ideas and can appreciate many different theories. INTPs can often do two or three things at the same time.

Potential difficulties

The less-preferred functions of INTPs are the introverted Sensing and extraverted Feeling. They usually find routine boring and may have difficulty remembering details and dealing with reality. INTPs often have lots of innovative ideas but may not implement them. They often have difficulty relating to people and understanding people's feelings. They tend to undervalue feelings that are incompatible with their thinking.

Communication

INTPs are open-minded. Their extraverted intuition enjoys brainstorming ideas or listening to other people discussing. INTPs are highly conceptual and they value precision with language. They often question the use of particular words and may appear pedantic. Because language has limitations some INTPs prefer to communicate with music. INTP language is global, analytical and questioning. They often find it difficult to express their feelings and find communication difficult with someone who is emotional. When trying to focus on what someone is saying they may seem distracted or may appear to be hiding something. Pressure from others to respond may interrupt their thinking and slow the process. INTPs find closed minds irritating and small talk irrelevant. If you want to change their behaviour present your ideas unemotionally, then give them logical reasons and time to process what you say.

Relationships

In a relationship INTPs want freedom and support for what they want to achieve. They want someone who understands them and respects their need for personal space. INTPs need affection and caring but often feel uncomfortable with a lot of physical displays of affection. INTPs often relate to people on the basis of their expertise. They usually find close relationships difficult and would say that people at work usually don't know them at all. INTPs find it difficult to get to know a person until they trust them. Once they trust they can become very close, but when the trust is broken the relationship ends. For INTPs the Feeling function develops at midlife so they will often find it difficult to express their deep feelings or even to know what they are feeling before this time. They will often show that they care by wanting to help their partners solve problems and find solutions.

Learning

INTPs are perpetual learners, pursuing knowledge for its own sake. They are highly conceptual and use their extraverted Intuition to explore ideas and connections. Their introverted Thinking develops when they are children and enables them to logically evaluate information according to an internal model or framework. They need freedom to explore ideas, to pull them apart and criticise them in order to understand them. Because their thinking is introverted they will find it hard to explain in words why they arrived at a particular conclusion.

INTPs read continuously on almost any topic of a theoretical nature. They are attracted to learning in a variety of areas such as science, architecture, music, linguistics, English, history, languages, the liberal arts, and information technology. INTPs have a passion for knowledge and understanding, and for finding the truth. They like to solve complex problems and continually ask Why? or Why not? They will spend hours writing an essay to get it just right. In a classroom they become bored if the work is not intellectually challenging, and will lose interest totally if the teacher is not competent. INTPs set very high standards for themselves and others.

At Work

INTPs enjoy work that is intellectually challenging. They are lateral thinkers and want complex problems to solve. They need autonomy, to be free to work in their own way towards a solution. INTPs can see any situation from many angles and need to explore and share their ideas with others. They enjoy being creative and original. They need a lot of personal space, especially if they are working on something they don't like.

INTPs tend to overcommit themselves at work and may have many projects incomplete because they are always trying to improve on what they have done. They don't usually set goals so they need deadlines to work to in order to complete tasks. They may be indecisive about work issues and may have difficulty organising and filing information or materials. They often file in piles and can live with a high degree of untidiness. They often don't see the clutter. INTPs may sometimes appear critical of others but are usually more critical of themselves.

Careers

INTP's are often attracted to careers that involve research, theory, design or teaching. These may be in very diverse areas, especially science, mathematics, psychology, fine arts, environmental consulting, advertising, information technology, architecture, philosophy, music, hypnotherapy, university teaching and strategic planning.

Team Role

INTPs prefer to work alone but enjoy interacting and sharing ideas with others. In a team they are usually creative, calming and good strategic planners. They sometimes have difficulty communicating with other team members, and need people around who can attend to the details.

Leadership Style

INTPs do not usually seek leadership roles. They don't like directing others and will not force people to do things. In a crisis they assume leadership and make quick decisions. They lead by example and expect others to follow. INTPs are more comfortable as leaders than managers.

The strengths of the INTP are that they see the big picture, they can generate possibilities, can develop strategies to find solutions, they add clarity, and they encourage competence and autonomy. Difficulties may occur if they don't delegate some of the practical tasks, if they don't meet deadlines, or if they remain aloof and don't relate well to the people involved.

Stress for the INTP

Causes of stress

The INTP has basic needs for competence and intellectual freedom, and will often experience stress if their competence is questioned by themselves or others. Since INTPs prefer Intuition and Thinking, much of their stress will come from using the less-preferred functions, Sensing and Feeling.

Extraverted Feeling is usually the least developed function of the INTP and the one most likely to get out control under stress. INTPs often have difficulty dealing with strong emotions and may be frustrated by people who are controlling, inflexible or not logical. They may become stressed by situations or by people when reality conflicts with the theoretical model. INTPs usually have difficulty being too long with groups of people. INTPs prefer the open-ended possibilities of Intuition and often have real difficulty managing time and practical details. Deadlines are often useful for INTPs, however, deadlines will create stress if there is not enough time to do the job well.

Behaviour under stress

When stressed INTPs may have emotional outbursts, raise their voice or cry and generally behave in ways that are not rational. They will often become focused on the task, ignoring the people, or may become totally immersed in the problem that is causing the stress. They may become defensive and disruptive when stressed or they may withdraw to think things through.

If people don't deal with serious stress they may engage in unhealthy psychological games to reduce the effects of the stress. An INTP who is not coping with stress may shut out all emotions, dismissing them as irrelevant, and they may avoid situation where they feel incompetent. The unconscious reasons for this behaviour are to regain the feeling of being in control and being competent, and to appear competent to others. The long term effect of this behaviour is that a fear of failure will prevent learning and lead to incompetence.

How to reduce stress

INTPs will often use physical activity such as running or manual work to reduce stress. They need lots of personal space when stressed and often withdraw from the company of other people. They need time to clear their minds, regain the big picture, and look realistically at their achievements and competence. They often find it helpful to relax and do nothing, listen to music, or use meditation or chanting to relax. To be healthy and manage their stress it is essential that INTPs honour their basic need for competence.

Leisure and Recreation

INTPs spend a lot of time alone in quiet activities such as reading, music, exercise, gardening, walking, watching films, using computers, making tapestries or travelling to unusual places. INTPs often have diverse leisure interests such as drama and acting; reading; listening to or playing music, especially classical and jazz; attending lectures; individual performance sports such as snorkelling, squash, surfing or martial arts. For INTPs, their work is often play.

INTPs enjoy reading books that stimulate thinking, increase their knowledge and add to their internal models. They read widely, including areas of science, science fiction, philosophy, psychology, black humour, healing and metaphysics. The topics may include such things as how the mind works, how language use affects the brain, Quantum Physics, Quantum healing, Zen, the history of man and Chaos Theory. They will often read seven or eight books at the same time and many will gradually accumulate a huge personal library.

INTP Development

Childhood (6 - 12 years)

The INTP child is usually a solitary child, happy to be alone much of the time. The Dominant function, introverted Thinking, develops during childhood so INTP children will spend time observing and analysing as they develop their internal logic. They are often inspired by patterns in the natural world, such as the movement of a snail, the changing seasons or the behaviour of a person. INTPs are capable of abstract thinking and philosophical questioning at this age. They will question everything as they build an internal framework, trying to understand what they see. Other people may not recognise their logical process because it happens internally. Many INTPs at the age of 10 or 11 have been deeply offended by a teacher who questioned whether their work was original because it was so advanced for their age group.

Reading is usually a favourite activity of INTP children. They seek knowledge for understanding, often seeing the author of a book as more expert than parents or teachers. They usually enjoy using computers, surfing the internet or playing computer games. Other activities may include music or drama, fine arts, martial arts and sometimes sport.

Adolescence (13 - 20 years)

During adolescence INTPs develop their extraverted Intuition and show an interest in learning new things and sharing their ideas and models. They will spend a lot of time discussing something that interests them and are often seen by others as over-intellectualising everything. They may learn many new things at this time, but once they have mastered something they will often move on to something new. At this time INTPs may appear extraverted as their activity is focused more in the outer world, but they will still need time alone. Although they may interact a lot with others, they do not need to be around other people. They spend a lot of time daydreaming and will usually have difficulty meeting deadlines and keeping things in order in the physical world. INTPs need intellectual freedom and will resist control. They will respond positively to guidance from adults they respect as competent. They may find school frustrating if the work is not challenging enough and will often prefer to work on their own.

Early Adulthood (20 - 35 years)

During this period INTPs develop introverted Sensing. The quiet, logical personality of the INTP continues throughout adulthood, but now their attention turns to the inner world of reality, facts, details and sensory experience. They will focus on things other than the mind, such as health and physical fitness, possibly going to the gym or learning massage. They may take up a practical hobby like craft, sewing, interior decorating, gardening, travel or reading books about facts. They enjoy taking an idea and turning it into reality. They may find their memory for facts and details increases at this time.

Midlife (35 - 55 years)

At midlife INTPs develop extraverted Feeling. During this time they become more sensitive to the feelings of others. They will often become more tactful, sometimes sentimental and more easily hurt. Though they are more interested in personal relationships and intimacy at this time, they still find emotions a challenge. They are often interested in people's lives and how they cope and may try to help people by helping them to clarify what is important to them. As their Feeling function develops they also become more aware of how they feel and what is important to them. Their personal values will begin to have more influence on decision making than before.

ISFP

Order of Functions:	Dominant	Fi
	Auxiliary	Se
	Tertiary	Ni
	Inferior	Te
Temperament:	Artisan (SP)	

Strengths

ISFPs are reserved, gentle, caring, fun-loving and practical. They focus on people, supporting and encouraging them. They are adaptable, spontaneous, and natural negotiators. They need flexibility and freedom in life and work.

The Dominant gift of the ISFP is introverted Feeling, so their decisions tend to be based on deep personal values. They defend the rights of others and want to make a difference in people's lives. They do a lot of good that is not seen, labouring happily in the service of others. ISFPs like to spend a lot of time alone and do not like being the centre of attention. The supporting function of ISFPs is extraverted Sensing. They live in the moment and absorb a lot of detailed information from the world around them. They seek constant activity, often at a quiet pace.

Potential difficulties

The less-preferred functions of ISFPs are introverted Intuition and extraverted Thinking. Most ISFPs find it difficult to assert themselves, wanting to maintain harmony and please others. They find it difficult to logically convince others to support their cause. ISFPs prefer to do rather than talk and may act before thinking things through. They often put off unpleasant tasks and may not complete tasks if they lose interest. They may focus on the details and not see the big picture. ISFPs avoid being the centre of attention and may avoid success to avoid being singled out for praise.

Communication

ISFPs see much but share little. Their extraverted Sensing focuses on facts and reality in the present situation. They are observant, noticing and remembering details, including body language, but get bored with a lot of detail from others. They dislike long explanations, preferring to get to the point quickly. ISFPs are good negotiators and are often seen as peacemakers. Their language is realistic, friendly and literal. ISFPs feel vulnerable talking in front of a group, preferring one-to-one conversation. They often find it difficult to express their feelings around logical people, and prefer to ask questions. If you want to change their behaviour calmly show them how it is having a negative impact on someone, give them some alternatives and show them the practical benefits of change.

Relationships

In a relationship ISFPs want freedom, equality and a person they can trust. They want to be loved and accepted as they are. They are very sensitive to other people's feelings and will usually try hard to please others and affirm others. They also want affirmation, but often only need it from one person. They are vulnerable and easily hurt by others and will avoid confrontation by withdrawing.

ISFPs usually have many acquaintances but may often feel alone. Once they trust and open up they can become very close to someone. Their Feeling function is introverted so they find it difficult to express feelings or even to know what they are feeling. But, they are very clear about what they value. They often enjoy making things with their hands and giving them to someone special.

Learning

ISFPs learn by doing and memorising. Their extraverted Sensing gathers detailed information from what they can they see, touch, taste, hear or smell. In a classroom they may become bored if they don't have something to do and may become distracted and lose interest in their studies. ISFPs need quiet for concentration. They learn best in a supportive, friendly environment where the content is related to real life experiences and the learning has practical outcomes.

ISFPs enjoy practical or experiential subjects with hands-on learning such as sport, craft, botany, biology, performing and music. They often enjoy learning from films and videos. They will read about things that interest them, such as stories about real people or stories with lots of action. As children they will often find school difficult because they get bored with theory or with long explanations by the teacher. They may have difficulty when asked to explore the meaning of something or to imagine something they have not experienced. They would prefer to write about the reality.

At Work

At work ISFPs enjoy a crisis and the opportunity to use their troubleshooting skills. They need physical freedom, variety, flexibility and the opportunity to be spontaneous. They can work in a structure if there is some freedom within it. ISFPs are able to concentrate for a long time on things that interest them. They get bored with routine and prefer a job where no two days are the same. They like to be busy and to have fun.

ISFPs focus on the outcome. They will often negotiate to get what they want and may step outside of the boundaries or rules. They are not impressed by rules, hierarchy, position or status. They often question the rules if they don't make sense to them or if the rules conflict with their values. They will often ensure that the organisation acts with compassion. They may not finish a task if they don't see any point to it.

Careers

ISFPs are often found in careers that involve people, physical activity, troubleshooting or negotiation. They have a strong desire to make a difference in the world, so they often choose careers where they can help people in practical ways. This may include nursing, teaching, counselling, special education, childcare, small business, trades and hospitality. They also choose careers in sport, singing, music, drama or working with plants or animals.

Team Role

ISFPs add fun and encouragement to a team. They are good at motivating people and creating a relaxed harmonious work team. They like freedom to do things their way. They may have difficulty meeting deadlines and may have more than one task in process. Their behaviour may appear extraverted but they will find time to be alone.

Leadership Style

ISFPs don't often seek positions of authority or leadership, preferring to be in the background or second in charge. When they do find themselves in a leadership position they usually try to form a leadership team. They will focus on the people and on creating harmony in the team. They build one-on-one relationships and use them to provide motivation, support and coaching. ISFPs allow people to have some freedom, while they act as negotiator. They will often start a project, then find someone with the skills to keep it going while they move on.

The strengths of the ISFPs include the ability to mediate, to negotiate and to allow the group to contribute their ideas, and their ability to handle a crisis. Difficulties may occur if they are too friendly and accommodating to deal with conflict, or if they don't pay attention the big picture.

Stress for the ISFP

Causes of stress

The main causes of stress for the ISFP are conflict, being the centre of attention and loss of freedom. While contact with people is important to them, they can become very stressed if they are the centre of attention. Some ISFPs will go out of their way to avoid being in the limelight.

Much of the stress for ISFPs results from using their less-preferred functions, Thinking and Intuition. They dislike any conflict or confrontation and are irritated by critical, uncaring or aggressive people. The ISFP's need for freedom means that they are stressed by inflexible situations or people. They dislike being tied down or controlled by people or deadlines and usually dislike long-term projects. They may be stressed by theories that are not grounded in reality.

Behaviour under stress

When stressed ISFPs may feel hurt and may become very defensive and misinterpret other people's words or actions. Even a person's look may be interpreted as criticism. They will often lose their spontaneity and feel unappreciated, and may withdraw. The ISFP can become very anxious and under great stress may have panic attacks. If the inferior extraverted Thinking takes over ISFPs may have difficulty thinking clearly and may be critical of themselves and others. Sometimes, if very stressed, they may have angry outbursts which are exhausting for them.

If people don't deal with serious stress they may engage in unhealthy psychological games to reduce the effects of stress. An ISFP who is not coping with stress may resort to blackmail games such as boredom or serious depression, risky behaviour or hurting themselves to hurt others. The unconscious reasons for this behaviour are to experience excitement and freedom, or to punish the person who has taken away their freedom. The long term effect of this behaviour is that they often lose their freedom because of their behaviour.

How to reduce stress

The ISFP will often use physical activity, fun, risk taking or new experiences, to reduce stress. They will usually withdraw from the company of other people preferring to be alone. It is helpful for them to check the facts and be realistic about the situation, then use their internal values to decide what is the appropriate action, before they act. To be healthy and manage their stress it is essential that the ISFPs honour their basic need for freedom and action.

Leisure and Recreation

ISFPs often enjoy spending quiet time alone reading, taking a bubble bath or being with nature. They also love being with children or animals, and often feel more at home with children than with adults. They love nature and the outdoors and much of their recreation will involve being in water, walking along a beach or in the bush, playing sport or athletics. ISFPs often enjoy activities such as motorbike riding, line dancing, abseiling, riding in hot air balloons, hiking, tri-athlon, athletics, visiting street markets or just hitting a ball against a wall. ISFPs are often gifted athletes and are competitive with the sport more than other with people.

ISFP also enjoy indoor activities such as using tools or gadgets, cooking new recipes, crocheting, tatting, making patchwork quilts, sewing, playing music and performing, craft, practical jokes, and community service. ISFPs often enjoy reading or watching movies, preferring romantic stories, adventure stories or comedians such as Harpo Marx. For ISFPs life has to be fun. They say things like "Why talk? Let's do it."

ISFP Development

Childhood (6 - 12 years)

ISFP children are usually very quiet and eager to please. They are fun-loving and caring, and they enjoy being with other people or animals. ISFPs interpret language and instructions literally and trust what is real. During childhood the Dominant function, introverted Feeling, develops so ISFPs are usually sensitive and vulnerable to hurt. They seek approval from the important adults in their world. They dislike conflict and try to create harmony around them. ISFPs feel other people's pain and are affirming and supportive of others. During this time they begin to develop their personal values on which future decisions will be based.

ISFP children like to have fun and need a variety of activity. They will become bored quickly if they don't have something to do. The favourite activities for ISFP children often include individual sports such as athletics, swimming and team games; outdoor activities; collecting toys, rocks or cards about their heroes; assembling mechanical things; playing computer games; transformer toys and gadgets; practical jokes and magic tricks; acting, drawing, singing or playing a musical instrument. They usually prefer activities that involve people or animals, and enjoy time alone.

Adolescence (13 - 20 years)

During adolescence ISFPs develop their extraverted Sensing and are constantly active, taking in vast amounts of information through their senses. They gather facts and details about people. They will put a lot of energy into an activity until they lose interest. Their behaviour during this period is often very extraverted as their activity is focused more in the outer world, but they will still need time alone. ISFPs need freedom and action and will resist control. They will respond positively to guidance from adults who understand them and encourage them to be themselves. They are usually active and often have a good social life. They may find school frustrating because of the emphasis on theory rather than practical work. If a conflict arises they will often withdraw or keep their opinions to themselves to avoid unpleasant confrontation.

Early Adulthood (20 - 35 years)

At this time the Third function, introverted Intuition, develops. The quiet, fun-loving personality of the ISFP continues throughout adulthood, but now their inner reflections are times of inspiration. At this time they begin to trust their hunches. They focus more on possibilities for the future and big picture concepts and theories. They will pay less attention to the details and practical realities and may find themselves daydreaming and forgetting things. Some ISFPs may feel drawn to dream work or meditation as they explore their inner Intuition. During this period they may find that their creativity increases. They will usually have their best inspirations when they are alone.

Midlife (35 - 55 years)

At midlife ISFPs develop extraverted Thinking. During this time they usually become more assertive and more logical in making decisions. They may begin to make plans for the future and will feel a greater sense of freedom to be themselves and to take charge. They will be less concerned about offending others, realising that some people will be offended no matter what you do. Many ISFPs at this time find that they are more confident in their own judgement and have courage to stand up for what they think is right. They may show an interest in such things as managing their financial affairs, or managing a business or investing.

INFP

Order of Functions:	Dominant	Fi
	Auxiliary	Ne
	Tertiary	Si
	Inferior	Te
Temperament:	Idealist (NF)	

Strengths

INFPs are reserved, caring, creative and idealistic. They value people and their development above everything else and they attach meaning to life's events. They strive to make a real difference in people's lives and believe anything is possible.

The Dominant gift of INFPs is introverted Feeling, so their decisions are based on deep personal values. They are aware of underlying unspoken feelings in others such as fear, anger and sadness. They defend the rights individuals and support causes that align with their values. Their supporting function is extraverted Intuition so they enjoy discussions and appear extraverted when talking about things they believe in. They have bursts of inspiration and seek constant growth which leads to change.

Potential difficulties

INFPs dream the big picture but do not always follow through to achieve what they want. They often over-commit themselves and then have difficulty completing projects or meeting deadlines. When they are young their ideals often clash with the outer reality. The less-preferred functions of the INFP are introverted Sensing and extraverted Thinking. They may neglect details and practical issues, and often have difficulty being assertive, wanting to please others and maintain harmony.

Communication

INFP language tends to be global, positive, spontaneous and humorous, often a play on words. Their extraverted Intuition sees connections and wants to brainstorm ideas and values, to help them understand. Their Feeling function is introverted so they need time to reflect before they can talk about important issues. Once they have thought about what they want to say they may think they have actually said it. They tend to be good listeners, very sensitive to people's feelings. INFPs are reserved, preferring in-depth conversations with a person they know, or writing in diaries, journals or poetry. They dislike confrontation and small talk, and have difficulty with people who don't value people. If you want to change their ideas or behaviour speak to the heart, to values of growth and human potential, then explore the options for change.

Relationships

Relationships are central for INFPs. They want people to understand them and to accept them as they are. They need the freedom to be themselves in the relationship. They want affirmation and physical affection, but may only need it from one person. Solitude is essential for INFPs, so they don't need their partner around all the time. INFPs are very sensitive to other people's pain and may feel overburdened with people's problems.

INFPs can be easily hurt by others. They are often close to only a few people that they know well and trust. They tend to internalise everything and may find it difficult to express their feelings or even to know what they are feeling. However, they are very clear about what they value. Trust and loyalty are very important to them and, if they are violated the INFP will end the relationship. INFPs usually avoid confrontation by withdrawing, but will confront an issues if their values are violated.

Learning

INFPs are imaginative and highly conceptual learners. They like complexity, theories and concepts, but need to be inspired to keep interested. They are usually keen readers, have very good language skills and often excel in subjects where they are able to express their ideas in written form. They are more concerned with meaning than with facts and thrive if they have the opportunity to be creative. INFPs tend to work in bursts of inspiration, easily make connections and enjoy learning that stimulates the imagination and connects with their values.

INFPs often do well academically and they are attracted to learning in a variety of areas including the arts, philosophy, poetry, science, psychology, music, metaphysics, healing and writing. Their extraverted Intuition develops in adolescence, so they may enjoy group work to explore ideas but they often prefer to work alone. They may become very stressed if they become the centre of attention, even when receiving awards. In a classroom INFPs will lose interest quickly if the work is not challenging or if there is disharmony.

At Work

At work INFPs want people to feel good, to know they are valued and to reach their potential. They can be very focused on a task if they believe in its value. They like to work with theory to promote growth and create change, finding new ways to do things. They particularly enjoy helping someone to manage their own life and turn it around. INFPs need variety, flexibility and harmony, and may have difficulty meeting deadlines.

INFPs need autonomy, freedom to be themselves. Role and position are not important to them so, if the organisation becomes too authoritarian, they will rebel against it or simply ignore it. INFPs are nonconformists and clash with authority if their values are violated. They may have difficulty if they become overwhelmed with other people's pain or if they try too hard to please others and don't deal with conflict.

Careers

INFP's need to contribute to people's lives and help them develop. They are often drawn to church ministry, youth work, counselling, psychology, education, natural therapies, writing, song writing, healing and change management. They may become involved in politics or industrial relations to protect the rights of individuals. INFPs may change careers often until they find something they believe in.

Team Role

INFPs are flexible and committed team members who like to exert a positive influence on the group, and to inspire and harmonize the group. They work well in teams where there is harmony, flexibility and support, and where they have some autonomy. Difficulties may arise if they don't meet deadlines, if the structure is authoritarian, or if they are too sensitive to criticism.

Leadership Style

INFPs will take on a leadership role if they can be helpful to people but will often feel out of place. INFPs are not authoritarian, preferring to allow team members some freedom. They usually prefer to be in a supportive or mentoring role in a team, rather than be the leader, and seldom have any ambition to progress to the top levels of management. They focus on the people and on creating harmony in the team.

The strengths of INFPs include their ability to help others develop, to create changes that benefit people and to challenge the values of individuals and organisations. Difficulties may occur if their values conflict with others, if they neglect the practical needs of the organisation, if they do not assert themselves when necessary, or if they become frustrated by the imperfections in others or in the organisation.

Stress for the INFP

Causes of stress

INFPs need to have meaningful relationships and to know that they are valued and are contributing to people's lives. They will become stressed if they feel unappreciated or if their values are violated, by themselves or others. They need privacy and are stressed by prolonged periods of interaction in large groups.

Since INFPs prefer Feeling and Intuition much of their stress comes from using the less-preferred functions, Sensing and Thinking. INFPs often have difficulty being assertive and are stressed by people who are critical, inflexible, controlling, negative, or not open to change. They may feel intimidated by very assertive logical people, especially if the integrity of the INFP is questioned. INFPs tend to take on too many things and may become stressed by deadlines, by too much structure or by practical things like filing and sorting, or facts and figures.

Behaviour under stress

Extraverted Thinking is usually the least developed function of the INFP and the one most likely to get out of control under stress. When stressed the INFP may become over sensitive and defensive and may easily misinterpret other people's words or actions. They may have difficulty thinking clearly and may be critical of themselves and others. They will often feel inadequate and unappreciated. Under great stress INFPs may become very critical, dogmatic or sarcastic as their inferior Thinking function takes over. They may have angry outbursts or may withdraw or cry a lot. If this happens they lose energy and spontaneity and may become emotionally exhausted.

If people do not deal with stress they may engage in unhealthy psychological games to reduce the effects of stress. INFPs who are not coping may ignore the symptoms or repress their feelings and delude themselves into thinking they are coping. The unconscious reason for this behaviour is to hide their feelings from others or themselves, to avoid facing the issue. The long term effect of this behaviour is that it is difficult for them to have a really meaningful and honest relationship.

How to reduce stress

To reduce stress INFPs need solitude. They will often engage in physical activity such as walking or cleaning, usually alone. They often find it helpful to talk to someone or write in a journal to get clarity. To be really healthy and to manage their stress it is essential that INFPs honour their basic need for meaning and appreciation. It is often helpful to re-focus on the big picture and where they are making a difference in the world.

Leisure and Recreation

INFPs enjoy a variety of leisure activities, preferring activities they can do alone or with a few people rather than large groups. They enjoy learning something that will help people or will help them to understand people. Their interests may include listening to music, song writing, writing poetry, photography, journal writing, daydreaming, movies, metaphysics, healing, art, dinner with a few friends, retreats, unstructured travel, jogging, swimming or Tai Chi. If they play sport it is for participation rather than for outcomes such as winning. Special hobbies like photography they will usually only share with someone who shows an interest.

INFP reading will focus on understanding people, the search for meaning and the search for wholeness. They often enjoy history and anthropology, poetry, family-oriented stories or stories with psychological themes. They may read such things as Quantum Physics or books about values in organisations. INFPs will often read the sections that interest them first, rather than reading from cover to cover. They often enjoy subtle British humour.

INFP Development

Childhood (5 - 12 years)

INFP children are reflective, sensitive, imaginative and obedient. The Dominant function, introverted Feeling, develops at this time, so INFP children are caring and vulnerable to hurt. They feel other people's pain, dislike conflict and try to create harmony around them. They seek approval from the important adults in their world, and are eager to please them. During this time they begin to develop the personal values on which their future decisions will be based. They often have a well-developed conscience and will question attitudes and any behaviours that ignore people's rights.

INFP children enjoy creative activities such as reading, art, music, creative writing, diaries, dance and drama, as well as activities that connect them with nature. They may take on an activity such as playing the piano to please someone. INFPs usually have difficulty paying attention to practical tasks and are easily bored with routine. In the midst of sport or practical games they will often find themselves daydreaming.

Adolescence (13 - 20 years)

During adolescence INFPs develop extraverted Intuition and spend a lot of time in activities that stimulate the imagination. They enjoy new and creative things and discussions about values. They often appear extraverted as they focus more on the outer world, but they still need time alone. INFPs read a lot and spend time daydreaming about the future. They are often spiritually-oriented and have a strong sense of vocation to heal the world or help humanity in some way. Most INFPs have a few close friends and usually do well at school. INFP males may not fit the male stereotype and may feel different or left out at this time. They may find it difficult to assert themselves, and may withdraw and not say anything to avoid an unpleasant confrontation. INFPs need autonomy. They will respond positively to guidance from adults who understand them and encourage them to be themselves.

Early Adulthood (20 - 35 years)

During this period INFPs develop introverted Sensing. The reflective, idealistic personality of the INFP continues throughout adulthood, but now their attention turns to the inner world of reality, facts, details and sensory experience. They focus more on their health issues and on practical activities. Many INFPs at this time will become involved in such things as art, craft, massage, meditation, natural healing, gardening, housework, or even furniture restoration or an exhilarating sport like skiing. Some will be drawn to prayer and meditation as a new source of inspiration. INFPs now will be more comfortable living in the present moment. Many INFPs will still find public speaking or being the centre of attention difficult, so they have to adapt to the demands of work and public life.

Midlife (35 - 55 years)

At midlife the INFP develops extraverted Thinking. During this time they become more assertive, more logical in making decisions and less concerned with harmony. They may even appear aggressive as they begin to take charge of their own lives and feel a greater sense of freedom to be themselves. Personal integrity is important to the INFP. Values are still the priority and they continue to fight for the rights of others. They also begin to realise that peace at any cost is not peace at all. Some INFPs at this time look for new challenges in work or the academic field. They may have a complete career change, setting up business ventures or beginning study in psychology, business or management. They will now be more confident in expressing their opinion and in making decisions.

The 16 Types Table

ISTJ	ISFJ	INFJ	INTJ
ISTP	ISFP	INFP	INTP
ESTP	ESFP	ENFP	ENTP
ESTJ	ESFJ	ENFJ	ENTJ

Identifying Your Own Personality Type

If you would like to identify and understand your own personality type it is advisable to receive feedback from a trained professional. Feedback can be given in a group setting or individually and will include completing a personality type questionnaire. If you would like information about how to contact a trained professional in your area contact the institute for Type Development (Australia) or choose one of the links on our website.

Institute for Type Development:
P.O. Box 715 Cherrybrook NSW Australia 2126
Telephone: 0417661104   International: +61 417661104
Website: www.itd.net.au   Email: type@itd.net.au

Useful References

Berens, Linda. (2000) *Understanding Yourself and Others: An Introduction to the Four Temperaments,* Huntington Beach, CA: Telos Publications.

Brue, Suzanne. (2008) *The 8 Colors of Fitness*, Delray Beach, Florida: Oakledge Press.

Delunas, Eve, (1992) *Survival Games Personalities Play*, Carmel CA: Sunlink Publications.

Hartzler, Gary & Hartzler, Margaret. (2005) *Functions of Type,* Huntington Beach, CA: Telos Publications.

Keirsey, David. (1998) *Please Understand Me II: Temperament, Character, Intelligence.* Del Mar, Calif.: Prometheus Nemesis Book Company.

Killen, Damian & Murphy, Danica (2001) *Introduction to Type and Conflict.* Palo Alto, CA: CPP.

Kroeger, Otto & Thuesen, Janet M. (1988) *Type Talk*, New York, NY: Delecorte Press.

Kroeger, Otto & Thuesen, Janet M. (1988) *Type Talk at Work*, New York, NY: Dell Publishing.

Lawrence, Gordon. (1993) *People Types and Tiger Stripes, Third Edition.* Gainsville FL: Centre for the Applications of Psychological Type. (teaching).

McGuiness, Mary. (2013) *121 Frequently Asked Questions about Psychological Type and Type Instruments.* Sydney: MaryMac Books.

McGuiness, Mary. (2007) *My Personality*, Sydney: MaryMac Books (for children).

Murphy, Elizabeth. (1992) *The Developing Child: Using Jungian Type to Understand Children.* Palo Alto, CA: Consulting Psychologist Press.

Myers, Isabel, (1980) *Gifts Differing*, Palo Alto, CA.: Consulting Psychologist Press.

Myers, Katharine D., & Kirby, Linda K., (1994) *An Introduction to Type Dynamics and Type Development,* Palo Alto, CA.: Consulting Psychologist Press.

Pearman, Roger. (1996) *I'm Not Crazy, I'm Just Not You.* Palo Alto, CA: Davies Black Publishing Co.

Tieger, Paul & Barron-Tieger, Barbara. (1992) *Do What You Are: Discover the Perfect Career for You through the Secrets of personality Type.* Boston MA: Little Brown & Co.

Tieger, Paul & Barron-Tieger, Barbara. (1997) *Nurture By Nature.* New York City, NY: Little Brown & Co. (about children).